FOR**GIVE**

FOR

REAL

SIX
STEPS
TO
FORGIVING

TIMOTHY L. SANFORD, M.A.

FORGIVE: For REAL
Six Steps to Forgiving

Requests for information can be addressed to:

Info@LifEdvice.com

Editing by Aarin Harper
Cover art by Dan Van Oss, Covermint Design
Interior Diagrams by Timothy L. Sanford

ISBN 978-1-0938-8080-9 (paperback)

Published by LifEdvice

Contents

PART II   93

APPENDIX

Introduction

When I was initially asked to write on the subject of forgiveness my first thought was, *"Hasn't there been enough books, seminars and sermons on it already?"* Besides, all you have to do is look it up in the dictionary, right?

Still, I was pretty sure there might be more to forgiveness than we've understood before. I asked myself a few questions: Do we truly understand what forgiveness is? Do we really comprehend the different aspects of our minds, hearts and souls it actually impacts? Do we truly know how to forgive using practical do-able steps?

After listening to all the people in my private practice office who have been given partial, misguided, inaccurate or down-right foolish information about what it means to forgive and "how to" forgive another person, I realized we do need another book! I've heard all sorts of clichés used on the topic and process of forgiveness in the course of everyday conversations. We may talk about it, dance all around it, throw out quick-fix answers about it but we still don't understand the depths of what forgiveness truly is. Not really.

My passion is for truth, and on this critical topic, there needs to be more accurate information shared when it comes to understanding and addressing forgiveness. There's more to this topic than meets the eye.

I'm a licensed professional counselor in the state of Colorado with over 29 years of experience. I've studied the issue of forgiveness for years so I could give my clients assistance with this subject.

I'm also an ordained minister. I've been in and around church, clergy and ministry environments for most of my 60 years. I've spent a considerable amount of time studying this matter from the theological, as well as the psychological, point of view. Talking about forgiveness in nice psychological—or even theological—terms keeps it sterile and at a safe distance, disconnected from our hearts and minds. The reality is it's *not* nice ... sterile ... or safe. It's *not* cheap, quick or easy either. When you look deeply at the issue of forgiveness, you touch, feel, see and smell the pain and woundedness that was inflicted by a person's wrong actions; actions that create the need for forgiving in the first place. Forgiveness and pain have a common denominator: wrong action by someone.

Wrongs come in all shapes, sizes and situations:

... Your three year old son steals a dollar bill from the top of your dresser.
... Your father walked out of your life when you were 10 years old.
... Your spouse had an affair with your "best friend."
... Your missionary father is so involved in "serving the Lord" that he's emotionally unavailable to give you the validation you need as a child.
... You are falsely accused at work and lose your job.
... Your husband physically and verbally assaults you regularly and threatens to take the children away and have you "committed" if you ever try to leave.
... Your father repeatedly molested you sexually for the first 13 years of your life.
... You were tortured and sodomized by a kidnapper or a group of crazed men.

Care to add your story to the list?

Events like these, from small to beyond comprehension, from obvious to subtle, happen to real people in all walks of life. These wrong actions are accompanied by proportional amounts of pain. Pain that can come in all different forms: some noticeable, some hidden, some physical, some emotional, some go all the way to the soul. Some pain is lingering, some eventually heals and subsides. Some wrongs cause a pain that is permanent, chronic and/or debilitating. Some pain never completely goes away. Let me say this again because it's so important and so ignored by most people—especially people in religious communities—some pain never completely goes away. Whether we like that reality or not, it's true and there when we discuss forgiveness openly and honestly. The very real

6

component of pain is very present when talking about forgiveness.

We often experience our pain through emotions. Feelings of sadness, disgust, anger or even rage, terror and/or helplessness. Don't trivialize this issue of forgiveness. These are real emotions. They're here for legitimate reasons. They may be emotions you remember having when the event took place. They may be feelings you have now as you look back at the event that caused the pain.

You're not wrong to feel what you feel. We need to look at "what is." There's no need to edit your feelings. There's no reason to acknowledge only the acceptable emotions nice people are supposed to have while stuffing the rage or disgust you feel inside. When you're considering forgiving, it's time for honesty. You can't put the pain in a sterile box and look at it from a distance.

The word picture that comes to my mind is that of entering into a hospital that's full of broken hearts, shattered dreams and expectations, wounded spirits and aching souls. The pain you experience is a result of wrong actions inflicted upon you. We need to tread lightly and with gentleness in this hospital because you and me—real people—are fragile and here to be treated and hopefully healed. We can't minimize and ignore the pain, it would be like slapping Band-Aids on broken femurs or giving aspirin to cancer patients. We can't afford to quote, "All things work together for good," or say glibly, "What doesn't kill you makes you stronger." Simplistic treatments, just like Band-Aids and aspirin in the cases above, don't help the broken hearts or the shattered souls lying in this hospital. This is *not* the right place or time for such comments, no matter how sincere they are.

Not now, not yet anyway.

First things first. You should know…

*Forgiveness is a journey that will take time …
maybe a long time to complete.*

Not a Place to Take Up Residence

The word picture of a hospital with hurting people can be used to describe the difference between being a *victim* and being *victimized*. Being a victim is a perception of yourself and can become your identity. You feel like a "victim." You act like a "victim." You believe you're a victim of this or that, or circumstances, or others, or whatever is outside of yourself. Identifying as a victim is the same as saying you choose to permanently live in the hospital unit.

No, don't do that. This is not a place to settle in and stay.

Being victimized however, is an honest statement and perception that admits something bad—wrong—happened to you. It's not you, but an incident that occurred. It means you were placed in this hospital by no choice of your own and you have no intention of taking up residence here. You're here to get better and then get out.

Hear the difference? When you hear somebody say, "I refuse to be a victim," that's what they mean. That person was wronged and wounded, but they refuse to stay in this hospital one day longer then they need to. They will heal. They will move on. This is their perception of themselves and the situation and it's an accurate one.

I don't know you personally or why you're reading this book. I don't know the wrong thing(s) that happened to you. I want you to be forewarned that the subject of forgiveness may elicit emotional responses in you. If you find yourself having a strong reaction to something, acknowledge the emotions. Search out what you're responding to and try to understand why. Understanding your reaction to what you're reading may be as valuable as the content itself. And if you don't have strong emotions … that's fine too.

I have no intention of putting you into a box or stereotyping you. Be careful not to put yourself into a box either. Some people had a father or mother abandon them when they were children. Some lost jobs for reasons that weren't their fault. Some have survived torture and others have been sodomized. You may—or may not—be one of these people. I don't know. The wrong done to you, that wounded you, affects you uniquely.

This book walks us through that hospital full of broken hearts, bodies and souls. If you're lying in one of these hospital beds, I respect you. I want to bring hope and a way of healing that's real to people like you and me. If you chose to walk beside me through this hospital, welcome. I hope you learn more deeply how to help yourself, and hurting people you come into contact with, to learn how to FORGIVE FOR REAL.

On a personal note, since I'm both a therapist and a minister, I write from both points of view at the same time—psychological and theological. If you hold firmly to a theological perspective and are leery of anything from the world of psychology, I don't think anything in these pages will offend you. When I quote from the Bible, I've put the references in the End Notes for reference purposes.

Likewise, if you're psychologically-minded and have little or no interest in anything theological, I hope the same is true for you. I don't think there's anything I say in the following pages that you'll find inaccurate. Please feel free to skip over the comments that are theologically based and please, don't get derailed by them.

Know too, I was not always the one walking around helping others who were hurting and wounded. I, myself, have been a patient in this hospital with my own heart, body and soul, wounded and broken. I understand the pain, confusion, anger and hopelessness well. In saying this, I'm sharing that I've also walked this journey and learned how to FORGIVE FOR REAL.

Whatever your personal background is, forgiveness is forgiveness. What's real is real and we need to approach forgiveness with that in mind. That's the way this book addresses the topic of one person forgiving another person.

How to FORGIVE FOR REAL.

Editorial Note:

This work began as a book with a separate workbook. After several discussions a decision was made to blend both into the one book you now hold.

At the end of each chapter you will find a Workbook Session. Each Session is designed to help you process what you read. Questions and activities will help you work the steps of FORGIVE FOR REAL one at a time. The Sessions serve as a guide to help you identify your thoughts and feelings about the material presented. From time to time you will find a **Head and Heart Check** question that encourages you to explore and identify your own motives and/or perceptions about a particular topic.

You may complete each Workbook Session when you finish reading the corresponding chapter. I'd like to suggest, however, you read the entire book first, then re-read the book and complete the Workbook Sessions. The flow and specific questions may make more sense to you that way, however, feel free to use the Workbook Sessions in the way that best suits you.

You have permission to make copies of any Worksheets as needed for your personal use.

With that said, here's how to FORGIVE FOR REAL.

Chapter One

Why Forgive?

Why Forgive?

Before you decide this is a silly question, think it over. What's the *reason* for forgiving another person, really? *Why* is it so important to understand and understand completely what forgiving is? I mean, deeper than doing it because you're supposed to ... or because you're told to ... or because ... well, you really don't know why but you're supposed to do it, just because. What is a real live-able *reason* to forgive?

I see a two-part answer to the "why?" question for forgiving.

1. It disconnects you from the wrong so you can heal.

Forgiving the other person who wronged you is a choice. That may sound obvious but it means you also have the choice not to forgive that offending person. So why would you choose *to* forgive? Because choosing *not* to forgive keeps you connected to the hurt, pain, injury and wrong done against you. This continued connectedness to these things impacts every part of your life, directly or indirectly. Whether you realize it or not, choosing not to forgive also keeps you connected to the person who hurt you and you're not free from their influence over you.

Not forgiving can give you a very strong illusion of safety and/or power. I say "illusion" because you may think holding on to the wrong keeps you safe. Not forgiving—so the illusion goes— helps you to keep it straight in your mind that "they" are the bad guy and you're the good guy. Not forgiving helps keep the anger alive, which gives you a sense of power you use to ensure you won't ever get hurt again.

But it's still an illusion.

Like glue, you're stuck to the hurt and to the abuser and carry both around with you wherever you go. You're not genuinely safe. Not really.

You've probably heard the phrase "let it go." But why? Because forgiving disconnects you—it frees you up—from the person, the event and the damage that was inflicted upon you. When you "let it go," you're freed up to heal and move on in life under your own control.

Think of it this way, every time someone wrongs you they push a suitcase of hurt and damage into your arms. Some suitcases are little tote bags while others are the size of a steamer trunk. As you go through life, people wrong you and give you a suitcase to carry ... one here ... one there ... another one over here ... what's going to happen if you keep all the suitcases and never "let (them) go," put them down or disconnect from them? Get the picture? You'll be bumbling through life banging into everything and everybody and unable to move about freely. Sooner or later you'll be buried under the massive pile and weight of the suitcases you've accumulated over the years.

This being "buried" may feel very normal to you because it's all you've known. However, walking through life juggling a number of suitcases will reveal itself in damaged relationships, depression, burn-out, anger, refusal to trust anybody ever again, isolating yourself, hatred, bitterness, addictions, anxiety, cynicism, perfectionism or any number of physical, social, emotional or spiritual symptoms. You may keep your outward appearance "together" (whatever *that* means) all the while you're buried alive. All of this is because you're still connected to the offense and the offending person. Forgiving disconnects you from both, the offender and the offense, and gets rid of the suitcases that are threatening to bury you.

I've traveled a lot and to travel well means to travel light. In order to travel lightly through life, you need to be able to forgive and disconnect from the baggage people dump on you. When you can travel light, you are more agile and can engage in authentic ways using healthy boundaries. Healthy boundaries act to keep you safe. No illusions. Real freedom.

Yes, this is easier said than done.

Let's get back to our original question. So *why* forgive? Forgive for survival, health, lightness and safety of mind, body and soul. That's why.

2. It keeps you from playing god.

There's a spiritual reason to forgive as well, but it's more than a "because God told you to" sort of thing. As a quick review, here are a few scriptural texts that talk about forgiveness:

> "For if you forgive men when they sin against you, your heavenly Father will also forgive you. But if you do not forgive men their sins, your Father will not forgive your sins."
>
> "And when you stand praying, if you hold anything against anyone, forgive him, so that our Father in heaven may forgive you."
>
> "Do not judge, and you will not be judged. Do not condemn, and you will not be condemned. Forgive, and you will be forgiven."
>
> "Be kind and compassionate to one another, forgiving each other, just as in Christ God forgave you."
>
> "Bear with one another and forgive whatever grievance you may have against one another. Forgive as the Lord forgave you." [1]

It's clear we're to forgive—but *why*? What's the reason behind these admonishments? Think with me here. *Why?* What's the *reason* God places such an importance on you forgiving the person who wronged you to the extent that He would withhold forgiveness toward you if you hold out and don't forgive? I'm asking these questions for a reason. You need to be sure of your reasons for doing what you do and know why you do the things you do. It's important for you to have good answers to the hard questions like, "How do I forgive my father for molesting my five year old daughter?" Do you have an accurate and truthful answer to this question? Do you have an answer that will touch the pain in your soul? Do you have an answer void of platitudes and clichés? Do you? This is why the *why* question is so important.

Remember, when we deal with forgiving we're dealing with wounds and pain. Please, be gentle, yet accurate.

Back to our second point. *Why* is forgiving so important to God? The short, blunt—and accurate—answer is because if you don't forgive, you make yourself out to be god and that causes a division between you and the real God.

> "No way. I'd never set myself up to be God. How can you say that?"

But you do. Follow the progression here:

> If you don't forgive the offending person …

> > You hold the debt over them …

> > > That makes you the debt collector …

> > > > Since God alone is Judge and the true debt-collector, you take over God's job and place …

> > > > > And you make yourself out to be god.

That's what you ultimately do, whether you do it knowingly or not. That's what happens if you don't forgive. You may be able to cover it up with the right lingo, even pretend to forgive, but you've set yourself up in opposition against the very God you say you want to get closer to. There will always be a tension and a distance between the two of you that you can't span, no matter how hard you try. This is why forgiving is such a big deal to God.

Additionally, God knows that if you don't forgive the person who wronged you, it keeps you wounded (God knows the first

14

reason too). God knows you were wronged. He knows you were injured. He knows the extent of the damage, great or small, and He doesn't want you to see how many suitcases you can carry through life. He provided a way out—a healing way—a way of disconnecting from the hurt and the baggage of the wrongs done against you; a way to be free. That way is called forgiving.

"Then you will know the truth and the truth will set you free." [2]

That's the *why* for our second point. That's *why* forgiving is so important to God and so important for you to understand correctly and deeply.

You don't have to do this by yourself. God desires—even aches—to walk with you. He knows the path, the sequence and the timing of things. He knows the illusions and the hidden tactics you use to keep from being hurt again. It is God who will help you the entire way. He's the Great Physician who will personally attend to your woundedness and broken soul. It is God who will teach you healthy boundaries so you can feel safe again … or for the first time ever.

That's the two-part reason to forgive for real.

You're On a Journey

Forgiving can't be formulized. It doesn't work that way. While there are specific steps to the process, you can't press a journey into a controlled schedule or regimen. A journey is individual, uncertain to some extent, with ebbs and flows, and unique to that person, time and situation.

---

journey \ *jer* ney \: (1) traveling from one point to another; (2) the path you take to get from where you are to where you want to end up.

Forgiving operates on what I call "heart time." The physical healing of a broken arm takes the time it takes to heal. A medical professional can make an estimate—assuming we know and have an accurate medical history—of the time frame it will take to heal but it's just that ... an estimate. Heart time will take the time it takes. Please don't force yourself—or anyone else for that matter—into a formula or a timeline.

Lastly, we can't oversimplify forgiveness, because it's *not* simple. It often gets interwoven with many other factors; a desire for justice, the whole issue of safety (a topic worth an entire book of its own), feelings of revenge, what about mercy, a desire to have the "good guy" win, wanting the "bad guy" to get his due, wishing for restitution for a life that's been drastically altered forever.

Angie's Story

I remember when a teenage girl, I'll call her Angie [3], entered my office one Tuesday afternoon for her appointment sporting a black eye. As a fairly observant therapist, I asked her how she got the shiner. She said she and her father had gotten into a physical fight (not the first time) the Saturday before. The reason for the fight? Angie's father was angry at her for unacceptable grades on her report card.

Excuse me!

There's more ... dad said he was totally in the right because he's the head of the house and she "started" the arguing in the first place.

Excuse me!

Add to that, Angie's mother watched it all, admitted it occurred and did nothing.

Excuse me, again!

So what's Angie to do? What's she to think about her father? Her mother? Who's she to be angry at: dad, mom, God or all of the above? Does she tell the youth leader at her church? Does she dare? Does God even care, really? If He does, why would He allow this to happen in the first place? Who wronged her: her dad, her mom? Was it really wrong in the first place? Who is she supposed to forgive … and for what? Was she wrong for defending herself and fighting back? Where's the justice?

Go ahead, tell Angie forgiving her father is easy. Tell her to, "just let it go." Tell her, with a compassionate look on your face, "What doesn't kill you makes you stronger." Is that what you're going to tell this teenager? Will that help this girl who's full of pain and disillusionment?

I don't think so.

Is that what you'd want to hear if it was you with the black eye? Would any of those platitudes help you in any way?

I didn't think so.

Have you ever told those things to another person?

I hope not but many have.

Did it really help them?

Angie and I began her healing journey. Angie chose to make the journey. She chose to stick with it even when it got hard. It took a long time but she did heal. She did forgive her father and her mother. She did move on with her own life. Even after forgiving her father, she didn't end up trusting or even liking him.

Like Angie, this is a journey you may choose to ask someone to take with you; a friend, a therapist, a minister, a mentor. Just a suggestion.

What is forgiving for real?

Ask 10 people to tell you what it means to forgive and you're likely to get 14 different—and usually very vague—answers. It's not clear. Even with all the books, sermons, seminars, etc. on forgiving, it's still not clear *what* it is and *how* to do it.

Here we go with defining and understanding this thing called forgiving.

Current English dictionaries will give you a definition of forgiving that goes something like this. Forgive is to:

> Pardon
> Remit a debt
> Cease to resent
> Stop considering it an injury.

This is a good start but I wanted more. I needed my understanding to be deeper. My clients needed more too.

For this, I went to the ancient Hebrew language, the language of the Old Testament portion of the Bible. In the Hebrew the root word for forgive means to:

> Burn
> Carry away
> Bear or endure
> Pardon from penalty

Okay, I get this.

> It also means to: suffer. [4]

What? When I first researched forgiveness, I was not expecting this at all. I double-checked and yes, the idea of "to suffer" is at the core of the Hebrew word we translate forgive.

My next step was to research the ancient Greek language in which the New Testament part of the Bible was written. (I had one year of Greek back during my theological training and frankly I didn't do so well). The word for forgive in Greek means to:

> Forsake
> Lay aside
> Leave
> Put away
> Yield up

Makes sense to me. Nothing really surprising here—so far.

The Greek word also means: to sustain damage. [5]

Again, I was shocked and didn't see this coming. And yet, sustaining damage is the very essence of what it means to forgive.

After synthesizing all my research, here's what emerged as a working definition of forgiving:

The Hebrew people had a religious ritual described in the Old Testament in which they used a "scape goat." This ritual was a physical display of the definition of forgiving we're talking about. It's this ritual where we get the phrase "scape goat" when we talk about a person who takes the fall and/or blame for others. The priests would symbolically "LIFT OFF" the sins of the people (the debt they owed to God) and place them on a goat. The priests and people would then "SEND IT (the goat) AWAY" from them—they would drive Billy (the goat) out of the city and into the wilderness. Billy would take the peoples' sins away from them and end up SUFFERING the damage from wild animals or weather.

That's it. That's what this thing called forgiving truly is. You (the offended party) LIFT OFF the debt from the offending party, you SEND IT AWAY and you (the offended party) SUFFER (ABSORB) the damage yourself. You don't absorb the *blame* or the *fault.* Not at all, and we'll see this clearly as we go through each step of this process. But that's it.

That's what it means to forgive for real.

The *offense* that needs forgiving is what evokes the emotions, opinions and pain you so deeply feel. The wrong action is what caused you to end up in this hospital hurt and wounded.

The *action of forgiving* that offending person, however, has nothing—really—to do with emotions, opinions or pain. The action of forgiving is judicial and takes place in a court of law. A courtroom can be used to illustrate this process. Forgiving is a type of legal transaction. While forgiving has its roots in the theological as well as the psychological worlds, it—at its core—is a legal transaction between you (the offended party) and the other person (the offending party). Do emotions, pain and opinions enter into the courtroom? Often they do but it's not the *focus* of the court proceedings.

The Six Step Process of Forgiving Another Person

The court proceedings in forgiving have an order—it's not random, vague or driven by strong personalities or feelings. Forgiving can be laid out in six logical steps. The steps follow an order, but your individual journey may have you loop back around to a previous step from time to time—that's to be expected.

Here's an overview of those steps:

> Step One – Forgiving starts with a clear statement of the wrong done against you and by whom.
>
> Step Two – With every wrong done, there's a debt that's been incurred. The offending person owes you something.
>
> Step Three – Decision time. You will need to choose who will be the debt collector.
>
> Step Four – Your copy of the debt is marked "paid in full."
>
> Step Five – You absorb the damage so you can heal and move on.
>
> Step Six – You treat the offending party as forgiven. This doesn't mean you automatically trust them, like them, are reconciled with them or even have to confront them. You treat them as if they don't owe you anything, because they don't.

The situations in which you find yourself needing to forgive another person will vary. Here are a few examples:

20

1. The person who wronged you is asking you to forgive them. They may, however, be sincere or insincere with their request. A sincere request to be forgiven helps. It's the same journey and while still painful, may be a bit easier and lighter. Maybe or maybe not. We'll see.

2. The person who wronged you is currently in your life to a greater or lesser degree. The person may be a family member (nuclear or extended), a co-worker, a friend, etc. A wrong has taken place, you still have to interact with them, yet they are not repentant for the wrong done nor are they asking to be forgiven. There's also a possibility they aren't even aware they wronged you. This type of situation is often the hardest to manage because the frequent interaction with the other person reminds you of the pain and/or reminds you that you need to keep alert against being wronged again.

3. You have no idea where the person who wronged you is or if they're even alive. For example, maybe you were wronged by your roommate 40 years ago and you have no idea where she is today or the person who molested you was your great-uncle and he's now deceased.

Regardless of your specific situation, the order in the courtroom still applies and the journey remains much the same. In Part I, we focus on the action of forgiving; what the six steps are in detail and how each builds on the previous step. In Part II we look at topics addressing the relational elements between you and the offending party. We'll look at questions such as:

"Do I confront them or not?" and "How do I make that decision?"

"What happens if I confront them and they deny it?"

"What does reconciling look like?"

"Do I have to trust them again?"

Whatever situation you find yourself in, for now, let's focus on the act of forgiving. The court is in session; let's take the first step in forgiving.

The FORGIVE FOR REAL Workbook Sessions at the end of each chapter will walk you through each of the six steps as well as assist you in understanding what it means to forgive another person who's wronged you.

Workbook Session

Let's Begin

What did you think forgiveness would be like? In FORGIVE FOR REAL, Tim describes the setting like this: *"entering into a hospital that's full of broken hearts, shattered dreams and expectations, wounded spirits and aching souls—the pain inflicted upon you as a result of wrong actions done against you."* What part of this word picture fits your idea of pre-forgiveness? How?

_____

_____

_____

_____

_____

_____

_____

_____

Have people ever given you "quick fix" forgiveness suggestions or platitudes? Did this help? What would you rather they have said to you?

_____

_____

_____

_____

_____

_____

Head and Heart Check:

Have *you* ever given "quick fix" suggestions or platitudes to another person when they were hurting and needed to forgive somebody who wronged them? If so, what might you have said to be more helpful to them?

_____

_____

_____

_____

_____

_____

_____

_____

_____

_____

_____

_____

In your own words, how would you describe the difference between *being a victim* and *being victimized?*

_____

_____

_____

_____

_____

What are your thoughts about forgiving as an action that takes place in a court or legal setting?

_____

_____

_____

_____

_____

_____

_____

_____

_____

_____

_____

_____

_____

_____

_____

_____

_____

_____

_____

_____

_____

_____

_____

Why Forgive?

What are some definitions of "forgiving" you've heard?

_____

_____

_____

_____

_____

_____

_____

When talking about the reason to forgive another person the book states, "... *not forgiving can give you a very strong illusion of safety and/or power*" and *"Not forgiving helps keep the anger alive, which gives you a sense of power you use to ensure you won't ever get hurt again."* What are your thoughts about each of these statements? Do you agree or disagree? Why?

_____

_____

_____

_____

_____

_____

_____

_____

_____

What do you think about forgiving being a *journey* and it occurring in *heart time*?

_____

_____

_____

_____

_____

_____

_____

_____

_____

_____

_____

Have there been people who have tried to hurry you or pressure you to forgive the offending person and make everything better? What kinds of emotions did you have when you were being pressed that way?

_____

_____

_____

_____

_____

_____

_____

_____

The phrases: *to bear or endure, to suffer* and *to sustain (absorb) damage* aren't usually phrases that come to mind when talking about forgiving another person. What are your thoughts about these three phrases and how they relate to the root meaning of the word "forgive"?

_____

_____

_____

_____

_____

_____

_____

_____

_____

_____

What thoughts or mental images come to mind when you read these three phrases?

_____

_____

_____

_____

_____

_____

_____

_____

The two reasons to forgive are:

       1. It disconnects you from the wrong so you can heal.
       2. It keeps you from playing god.

That's fine, but what are *your* reasons for forgiving the person(s) who wronged you?

_____

_____

_____

_____

_____

_____

_____

_____

_____

_____

_____

How does each of the wrongs done against you keep you connected to the person who wronged you? Look carefully, because if you haven't forgiven, you *are* connected in some way. Write out what the connection(s) is/are.

_____

_____

_____

_____

_____

_____

_____

_____

Forgiveness is defined as:

> "TO LIFT OFF" the weight of the debt,
> to "SEND IT AWAY" from you,
> and to "SUFFER" (ABSORB) the damage or injury
> yourself.

What do you think of this definition? Are there parts of this definition you have a difficult time understanding or accepting? If so, why?

_____

_____

_____

_____

_____

_____

_____

_____

Head and Heart Check:

Forgiving keeps you from playing god, but have you ever wanted to play god? If so, why?

_____

_____

_____

_____

_____

_____

PART I

Chapter Two

State the wrong done	State the debt owed	Who will be the debt collector?	Mark the debt "PAID IN FULL"	Absorb the damage	Treat them as forgiven

The Wrong Done Against You

The first step in any court proceeding is to establish what wrong was done, what crime was committed, what law was broken. Emotions are set aside; personal opinions don't have a place on the stage. Even the fact of the pain this wrong inflicted is not the focus.

This isn't as easy as it might sound because things like emotions, personal opinions, beliefs and the presence of pain are the very things that can easily cloud your reasoning. The first step in forgiving is to figure out exactly what needs to be forgiven. If you have no clear sense of what wrong took place against you, how do you know what you're trying to forgive? You can't.

> *The more vague your understanding of the wrong,*
> *the more vague your forgiving is*
> *and*
> *the more vague and incomplete*
> *your healing will be.*

What a Wrong Is

We live in a society that claims, "You have your reality and I have mine." While that may sound enticing it's just not true or sound. Facts are facts. Reality is reality. Reality was here long before you or I were born and will be here long after we're both dead and gone. There's not a human being—living or dead— who has the power to say what is and what isn't reality. What each of us *does* have, however, is our *perception* of what is real.

Sanity is when your perception of reality and reality match. Insanity is when your perception of reality and reality don't match.

If I told you, "I'm a firetruck." Is that reality? Is that a fact?

"No, it's not reality, Tim. You're a human being, not a firetruck."

Oh, that's just *your* reality. *My* reality is I'm a firetruck.

"No, Tim, you may *think* you're a firetruck but you're really a human being."

There you go, trying to force *your* reality onto me. I have *my own* reality and my reality is as real as yours.

Okay, let's stop here.

What's *real*, am I a firetruck?

"No."

Why? Because you said I'm not?

No, it's because I'm *not* a motorized vehicle equipped to fight fires.

That's reality. That's real. That's a fact. Right?

"Right."

So, who's the sane one here, you or me?

Who would be considered insane here, you or me?

You're sane. I'm not. Right?

Why?

Your *perception* (Tim's not a firetruck) and *reality* (Tim's not a firetruck) *match*.

My *perception* (Tim's a firetruck) and *reality* (Tim's not a firetruck) *don't match*.

That's life. A "reality check." Get the idea?

So when we look at a wrong that was committed we'll probably need to wade through lots of people's perceptions of things to get to what's real.

You may need to wade through a lot of your own perceptions as well and do a reality check.

Easier said than done, yet critically important to do.

So, what constitutes a wrong? Let me lead you through the two stage process you can use to decide if an action is a wrong or not.

First stage:
The first question we ask is, "What civil law was actually broken?" Was there a crime committed? If so, there's the wrong. Plain and simple. If a civil law was broken, a wrong has been committed.

Second stage:
The second question we ask is, "What's the moral law or code that was transgressed?" Here's where the waters can become

muddy. Here's where people's *perceptions*—which are based upon their philosophy of life—come into play. Still with all the different and varied philosophies of life within our society there are some assumed moral rights and wrongs that have been understood for generations.

This is how we determine what is really wrong.

You might think it's clearer and easier to determine right and wrong from the theological perspective. Not really. There are as many opinions, beliefs, interpretations and philosophies that muddy the waters as quickly here as there are in any legal proceeding.

So how do you determine whether something is a wrong or not? In one of my theology classes I was taught this three-question process for determining what is actually morally right or wrong. I'll use the illustration of a bull's-eye target.

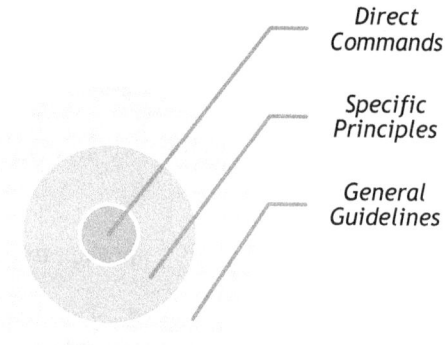

Direct Commands

We begin with the bull's-eye circle and ask, "Are there any *direct commands* that speak to this subject?" If there are *direct commands* in the Bible then breaking that command constitutes a morally wrong action.

Realize there two major ways a wrong can be done against you.

1. DOING something BAD to you. This is a more obvious form of a wrong and the one that gets our attention more quickly. Slapping you in the face and yelling at you when you were a child is DOING something BAD to you. You were the recipient of wrongful actions. In theological circles they call this a sin of commission.

2. NOT DOING something GOOD to you is as damaging but far less noticeable to you, the offending person, and others around who "witness" it. Neglecting you and refusing to acknowledge you even exist as a child is wrong. But how can you point at a NOTHING? You can't. That's my point. There's nothing to notice or "witness" because the GOOD thing that needed to happen DIDN'T. Theologians call this a sin of omission.

Friend: "So what bad thing(s) happened to you as a child? Were you abused?"

"No."

Friend: "So there you go, nothing bad happened to you, so there's nothing wrong with you. What are you whining about?"

This is exactly why most children assume it was their fault; because if they had been smart enough, good enough, tough enough, cute enough, something enough … then they would have gotten the love and attention a parent is responsible to give their child.

Neglect is more damaging to a child than active abuse. Think about that for a bit. Abuse says "I don't like you!" Neglect says "You don't exist!"

As you look for what wrongs were done against you, be sure to look for the GOOD things that are required from the person that weren't given to you. Both are wrongs done against you. It's the same level of wrong and damage just in very different forms.

What often happens in various religious groups is they make up their own interpretations of what is a command. This is usually done in order to bring a sense of power and control over parishioners and their behaviors. Once again, their *perceptions* (*interpretations* is what religious people like to call them) and the reality of what the Bible actually says don't always match.

And when perceptions don't match reality, what's that called?

Insanity.

This first question is the only one we need to be aware of since we're only concerned about deciding what wrong was committed, but here are the other two questions in the three-question process just so you have the complete information.

Specific Principles

If there's no *direct command* that speaks to the issue at hand, we move to the second circle out from the center and ask the next question, "Are there any *specific principles* that address this topic?" With *direct commands* there *is* a right or wrong conclusion but with *specific principles* it's not a matter of right or wrong but rather an issue of smart or foolish. It's many of these *specific principles,* however, that leaders and individuals attempt to smash into the circle of *direct commands* in order to make everything a right or wrong, black or white world for themselves and others
If there are *specific principles*, apply the principle(s) as best you understand and go on. In doing so, you may apply them differently than I. There's room for differences.

General Guidelines

If there're no *specific principles*, we move to the third circle out and ask the third question, "Are there *any general guidelines*?" If so, apply all the *general guidelines* as best you can and go on. Simple as that. Here—in this outer circle—is where there's the most space for differences, perceptions/interpretations and varied ways of applying *general guidelines*.

Since this a book on forgiving and not a theological discourse on how to understand what the Bible says about each and every subject, I'll end this discussion here. So, if it breaks a civil law, it's a wrong and if it breaks one of God's moral laws, it's a wrong.

What's Not a Wrong

There're lots of things that happen in personal relationships that cause pain that aren't wrongs and therefore don't need to be forgiven:

o   Forgetting your birthday.
o   Stepping on your foot as we're dancing.
o   Buying you the "wrong" kind of toothpaste.
o   Being late for an appointment with you.
o   Breaking your leg when tackling you during a football game.
o   Smudging your glasses.
o   Misunderstanding you wanted me to do this or that …
o   Bumping into you and knocking the boxes of cold cereal out of your arms.

All these things can cause some level of pain, disappointment or tension between you and me. But I did nothing *wrong* against you that I need to ask your forgiveness for.

This is why it can be hard for you to identify what wrong really did happen. You may find the event that didn't turn out the way you wanted or expected it to—that did cause disappointment, discomfort or even some relational pain—was not a *wrong* at all. Does it still need to be addressed to make the relationship open and whole again? Probably, but it's *not* something to be forgiven.

This can be especially true if the pain is great and we want somebody to "fix it" or "to pay." Follow this train of thinking:

If the person didn't do a wrong …

There's nothing they owe you …

Then there's nothing (no debt to collect) to hold over their heads ...

Which means, you have to "fix it" (absorb the cost) yourself.

This may not be what you expected or want—to be responsible to fix somethings yourself—but not everything that makes us uncomfortable or causes us "pain" needs to be forgiven

Forgiving is Not

Back to the court room and step number one. Forgiving is not forgetting the event ever happened. On the contrary, the court just documented that it *did* happen and the wrong *was* real and it needs to be dealt with.

Forgiving is not you saying, "Oh, it's okay" or "It's no big deal." The court just determined it *was* wrong and wrongs are *not* "okay." Wrongs, even small wrongs, *are* big deals because they're wrong.

Let me use the example of the man named Joseph in the book of Genesis. [1] His brothers hated him and devised a plan to kill him but decided at the last minute to sell him as a slave instead.

Any wrong committed here so far?

Yes. (Name the wrong)

The brothers then lied to their father about Joseph's disappearance.

Any wrong committed here?

Yes. (Name the wrong)

A number of years later, Joseph is the number two person, second only to Pharaoh, in the great land of Egypt, the only land that has food during a great geographic famine. The brothers leave their land of Canaan, go to Egypt to buy food and end up in front of their little brother, Joseph. After several events directed by Joseph to test his brothers, the time comes when he reveals himself to his brothers who, up until then, didn't know the great Egyptian was their little brother.

> "I am your brother, Joseph," great opening line, "the one you sold into slavery!"

> So, did Joseph *forget* the wrongs done to him?

> No.

> Did he say, "Don't worry, it wasn't that big of a deal"?

> No.

He *did* remember and he *didn't* minimize it. While the account doesn't say specifically, somewhere during those years in Egypt he forgave his brothers. How do we know he did this? He goes on to tell his brothers, "God has caused me to forget (stop mulling over) my trouble (the wrong, the pain, the grievance and impact of that wrong)." Joseph knew the wrong done against him. He understood the debt his brothers owed him. He chose to forgive and he was able to move on and be free.

> Did Joseph automatically trust his brothers?

> No.

He tested them—several times—before ever telling them who he was (more on this in Chapter Ten) and wisely so. The last time Joseph saw these men, they'd just sold him off for a slave. They weren't safe men then, were they safe men now? He didn't know. Trust is *not* automatic. Neither is confrontation or reconciliation, three topics that we'll address in Part II.

With forgiving, we begin here, stating what the wrong done against you was, as clear and as simple as you can.

Angie's Story

As an example of each of step, I'll walk you through Angie's journey.

If Angie goes to county court—which she did not [2]—the first thing the district judge decides is:

> Which Colorado Revised Statue was violated ...
> By whom ...
> And against whom.

The physical assault of another person is a crime. The judge just validated a wrong was committed. Outside of civil laws, is a father physically injuring his daughter wrong?

> Yes.

What's the job of a dad? What does God expect from a father? It's to protect and validate his children. That's the job description of a dad given to him by society in general and by God more specifically. Did Angie's father protect her?

> No.

Did he validate her even though he may not approve of her grades?
> No.

So a civil law was broken and a moral law was broken too.

Again, does the judge care if the grades were acceptable or not? No. Does he care that this specific father got angry at this particular daughter? No. What the judge—and the court—*is* concerned about, and focused on, is what *wrong* actually took place. This is court, not interpersonal relationship counseling. Make sense?

This father physically assaulted Angie and that was wrong.

Wait, is Angie's father the only person in this situation who wronged her? Think again. What's the mother's moral responsibility and obligation toward her daughter? Is her lack of action also a wrong action?

God's moral law expects a mother to protect and nurture her children. Did Angie's mother do that for her?

40

No.

Her mother's lack of action was an act of omission. This mother failed to protect her daughter and that was wrong.

I did with Angie what I do with most of my clients going through the forgiving process, I gave her a worksheet and had her physically write out the wrong(s) her father and her mother did against her. There's something about a tangible document staring you in the face that helps validate the wrong did happen and it's not your imagination. There was a wrong and it isn't just your opinion. Continuing with the legal word picture, everything in court gets documented. We're going to do the same on this journey of forgiving.

Don't Fight Reality

I often find that people tend to fight reality—in any number of ways:

> 1. They don't want the wrong to really have happened … they don't want it to be a real event in their life.
>
> 2. They don't want the offending person to really be the one who did the wrong. Often it's easier to accept the blame than it is to acknowledge the particular person as the one who's truly to blame for the wrong done.

Children almost always do this rather than see the fault belonging to their parent.

The other reason for accepting the blame on ourselves is because of thinking …

> If it *was* my fault …

> > Then that means I was still in control but just didn't make the right choice.

> But … if it *wasn't* my fault …

Then that means I was *not* in control of what happened to me …

Which means I was powerless …

And that's truly a terrifying situation.

3. They want something that wasn't truly a wrong to be a wrong. That way somebody else is responsible to fix the situation.

4. They don't want to admit they got taken advantage of. It's a huge embarrassment they don't want to face.

"How could I not see it coming? I can't believe I was so stupid."

5. They were taught it was their fault from a very early, vulnerable age.

6. They were taught "authority" is never wrong (even when authority actually was wrong—they were taught to believe that they were right).

These are some of the reasons why a person would fight, or misperceive, reality.

The problem is …

Whenever you fight reality … you lose.

Reality will always trump your wishes, hopes and/or illusions … eventually.

A wrong, is a wrong, is a wrong.

And if it happened to you, it happened to you.

And if it's the other person's fault, it's the other person's fault.

And if you were powerless to stop the wrong ... then ... yuck ... you were powerless then.

That's reality—not perceptions—that's reality.

Workbook Session

State the wrong done | State the debt owed | Who will be the debt collector? | Mark the debt "PAID IN FULL" | Absorb the damage | Treat them as forgiven

Step 1 - The Wrong Done Against You

*"Facts are facts. Reality is reality... **no one** has ownership of reality to say what is and what isn't reality."* What are your thoughts about such a strong statement?

_____

_____

_____

_____

_____

_____

_____

_____

Write out how you would explain "reality" to another person?

_____

_____

_____

_____

_____

How would you explain what "perceptions" are to another
person?

_____

_____

_____

_____

_____

_____

_____

_____

_____

"Sanity is when your perception of reality and reality match."
How does this statement sit with you? Why?

_____

_____

_____

_____

_____

_____

_____

How would you explain the difference between "perceptions"
and "reality" to another person?

_____

_____

_____

_____

_____

_____

So, using the context of the book, if I told you, "I'm a firetruck!" what would you think of me?

_____

_____

_____

_____

_____

_____

_____

_____

_____

_____

The book sets forth a narrow definition of what a wrong action is by asking: _"What civil law was actually broken?"_ and _"What's the moral law or code that was transgressed?"_ How does this definition sit with you? What is and is not sitting well? Why?

_____

_____

_____

_____

_____

_____

_____

_____

_____

What actions do you consider "wrong" but don't fit the book's definition of a wrong? Why do you think this action (or these actions) are legitimately wrong?

_____

_____

_____

_____

_____

_____

_____

_____

_____

_____

Head and Heart Check:

Do you want this action (these actions) to be "wrong" because you don't like them or you've been hurt by them before and think if something hurts you it deserves to be called a wrong? Why do you think they ought to qualify as a "wrong" action?

_____

_____

_____

_____

_____

_____

_____

What are some actions you have been taught are "wrong" but don't fit the criteria of breaking a civil or a moral law?

_____

_____

_____

_____

_____

_____

_____

Head and Heart Check:

If you like high structure, a highly regimented way of life, and think anything outside this way of life is "wrong", what needs do you want met by that kind of lifestyle? What do you hope to gain by living that way?

_____

_____

_____

_____

_____

_____

_____

_____

_____

_____

_____

What thoughts came to mind when you read, *"Whenever you fight reality, you lose"*? Do you agree?

_____

_____

_____

_____

_____

_____

_____

_____

_____

_____

Look at Worksheet 1 (Located at the back of your book.)

On Worksheet 1 list the names of the people who have wronged you. If you're not sure what happened was a wrong using the criteria from the book, put their name down anyway and you can sort it out later.

Here's what Angie's Worksheet 1 looked like:

Angie's Example:

Father

Mother

Once you think your list is complete, continue.

Get out Worksheet 2

Take the person's name from Worksheet 1 and put it at the top of Worksheet 2; one name per Worksheet 2 page.

You will work through the rest of the Worksheets for each name you wrote down on Worksheet 1.

People seem to do better when they work through the Worksheets one person at a time. Do what works for you. Go through the steps as far as you are able to, then put the Worksheets for that person aside and let things rest for a while. When you're ready, simply pick up where you left off.

On Worksheet 2 list all the wrongs you think this specific person from Worksheet 1 did against you. If you're not sure it was a legitimate wrong (meets criteria from the book), add it to the list anyway, you can sort it out later.

Angie:

Name of person: *Father*

    (1) He got mad at me over my grades.

    (2) He physically hit me and gave me a black eye during the fight   we had.

Test It:

Once you've listed all the wrong actions done against you, look over every entry and put it to the test:

    What civil law was broken?

What's the moral law or code that was transgressed?

Don't hurry this step. Be as clear and accurate as you can. If you're not sure the wrong action clearly passes the test of breaking either a civil or a moral law, it's probably not a legitimate wrong. If the action doesn't pass this test cross it out. If you're not ready to cross it off yet, put a question mark next to it so you know to come back to it and test it again sometime.

Angie:

---

(1) He got mad at me over my grades.

Remember, some actions that cause pain and hurt aren't wrong actions—foolish or stupid maybe—but not wrong. Foolish and stupid actions need to be *addressed* but not forgiven. No civil or moral law was actually broken. You may want something to be a wrong action but it may not actually be. Work through your list carefully and precisely.

This is *not* a civil wrong. It's *not* a moral wrong either. No law was broken by Angie's father getting mad over her grades. But … since her father *has* repeatedly treated Angie with contempt and anger for a number of years, it was apparent he did *not* validate/affirm Angie in the way a father is morally obligated to do. The wrong got re-stated to this:

Angie:

---

(1) He hasn't provided me with enough validation I've needed as his child.

Stating it this way, clearly identifies a wrong. This *is* a moral wrong because a key part of a father's job is to validate every one of his children and he didn't do his job. He didn't fulfill his moral obligation as a father to Angie.

Mark It:

For each legitimate wrong you have left on Worksheet 2, off to the side, mark it with a **C** for a civil wrong and/or an **M** for a moral wrong. You may need to think through the specific action to determine what the actual wrong is.

---

(1) He hasn't provided me with enough validation I've needed as his child.   M

(2) He physically hit me and gave me a black eye during the fight we had.   C and M

To make it easier to follow each wrong through the remaining steps, you may want to number each specific wrong you have listed. Once you're sure each of the wrongs listed are clear and legitimate, continue.

Chapter Three

State the wrong done → **State the debt owed** → Who will be the debt collector? → Mark the debt "PAID IN FULL" → Absorb the damage → Treat them as forgiven

The Debt That is Owed

The court determined a wrong was done against you and it's been documented.

With every wrong, with every crime that's committed, with every law that's broken, there's a debt the offending person becomes obligated to pay the offended person. Psychologically and practically this makes sense but in some theological circles this doesn't sound nice or loving or gracious, etc. etc. etc. It's still true—something is owed to the person who was wronged. This is the way the court system works. This is justice. This is the way God works. Once the wrong has been defined and documented, the next step is to determine what the offending person *owes* the offended person. This is called a debt.

What's the Debt?

When it comes to tangible items, it's easy to figure out the debt that's owed:

> If your son steals a dollar from you—he owes you a dollar.

> If a person lied to you—they owe you the truth.

> If a person lied about you to another person—they owe you the truth and they owe the person they lied to the truth about you.

> If a person totals your automobile in an accident that was their fault—they owe you the value of that vehicle.

"Yea right, but that's not how our legal system works these days."

That may be true but what I'm talking about is the way the court system was initially designed to operate.

But what does Angie do with her black eye? If your father left you when you were 10 years old, what does he owe you? How do you figure out the debt that is owed to you from being sexually molested by your father as a child? What's the debt the other person owes you when their false accusations about you caused you to lose your job?

Often we want the wrong fixed, a rewind, back to, "as if it didn't happen." How can you un-steal a dollar bill? How can you un-lie? How can you un-total the person's vehicle? How can your father un-molest you? It can't be done. This forgiving journey is not about making it, "as if it never happened." That will never be possible. Forgiving is about correcting or making some type of restitution for the wrong that happened so the offended person can go on with their life.

Step One takes time and effort to figure out, identifying the wrong, the law that was broken. Step Two takes just as much time and effort to understand; determining the actual debt that now exists.

Angie

Was it wrong for her father to be disappointed by her grades?

No.

What is wrong for her father to be angry toward Angie?

No.

Was it wrong to physically hit and injure her?

Yes.

The judge determined a wrong did take place; her father wronged Angie by physically assaulting her.

Now what does this father owe his daughter? What's the debt he has to pay? Angie's father can't un-blacken her eye. So what does he owe her?

When a person wrongs you in a less tangible way, here's what the person owes you: they owe you an apology—a confession—and whatever restitution can legitimately be made. Before your brain shuts down, hear me out. The apology I'm talking about has five specific components to it. Whether you collect on this apology or not can't be guaranteed. Even if the person refuses to give this apology—or in some cases the person is dead or nowhere to be found—this is still the debt they owe you.

> "But what good is it to have a debt owed to you when you know it won't ever be paid to you?"

That question will be answered in Step Three. Be patient.

Now comes the second court document, if you will. Angie and I worked out the actual debt her father owed her and wrote it down—making it tangible and official.

A Real Apology

A true apology from the offending person, given to you, the offended person, will have these five components. The offending person will state:

> "I", a personal admission that they actually—not maybe—were the offending person.

> "did this (name the wrong)...", a clear confession of the action that took place.

55

"against you …", a clear admission that you are the offended person.

"it was wrong …", a clear confession and admission that the action was actually a wrong action.

"it hurt you …" a statement acknowledging that the wrong action had a damaging and negative effect on you.

"and I will make whatever restitution I can." A statement accepting the legitimate debt incurred that is theirs to pay.

That's what the offending person owes you. There's no way they can undo the wrong done. The good news is you don't need it undone in order to heal and move on with your life.

And … if that offense resulted in hospital bills, they owe you the money for those bills too. If that identified offense landed you in a therapist's office, they owe you the money to pay the therapist. That's restitution.

That's the debt that's legitimately owed to you.

"Yes, but I'll never collect on that! My father will never admit he molested me. Never."

Whether your father ever gives you the apology or not—he still *owes* you that. Like I said, what to do about collecting that debt or not will be answered in later Chapters.

Back to Angie

Angie's father owes her the apology. Here's how that apology would sound if it had ever come:

"I (your father) physically assaulted you and gave you a black eye. It was wrong of me to do that and I realize how much it hurt you, physically and emotionally. I will

56

cover the cost of any therapy you need and I will buy you another lamp like the one I broke of yours."

There you have it. That's what is owed to Angie.

Will it un-blacken her eye?

No.

Like we said, forgiveness is not going to un-do anything. It's to help Angie heal from the offense.

"What about her mother?"

Angie's mother was able, after some time with us in therapy, to give her apology to Angie. Heart-felt and with some uncertainty in her voice, she was able to say to Angie's face:

"I didn't protect you from your father when you two got into that fight. That was wrong of me. I see (now) how not protecting you hurt you deeply. I am so, so sorry."

There's the apology that this mother owed her daughter. And she was able to give it to her.

With every wrong there's a debt owed. It's important on the forgiving journey to determine the restitution for that debt as clearly as possible.

Workbook Session

State the wrong done | State the debt owed | Who will be the debt collector? | Mark the debt "PAID IN FULL" | Absorb the damage | Treat them as forgiven

Step 2 – The Debt that is Owed

Worksheet 3

Look over each wrong done against you that's left on Worksheet 2. You can begin at the top, or wherever you choose, it doesn't matter. Here's where numbering each wrong on Worksheet 2 will help you keep track of things.

For each wrong you listed on Worksheet 2, write out on Worksheet 3 what the person owes you because of that wrong.

Angie:

On Worksheet 2 she listed:

---

(1) He hasn't provided me with enough validation I've needed as his child.   M
2) He physically hit me and gave me a black eye during the fight we had.   C and M

On Worksheet 3 then, for Wrong number 2, Angie wrote:

> *(2) He owes me a confession of what he did.*
> *(2) He needs to pay for the therapy I'm in trying to deal with all this.*
> *(2) He needs to pay for the doctor's visit to examine my black eye.*

Take your time on this step too because you need to be as clear, accurate and specific as possible.

Once you've written out everything the person owes you I encourage you to review it with another person you trust to double-check yourself. If you don't have another person to talk to, double-check it one more time yourself. Confirm that your details are as accurate as possible and the identified action is a legitimate wrong.

It's possible restitution has already been made by the person who wronged you. Go over the list on Worksheet 3 and put a **P** (paid) next to each debt owed that has been paid. If restitution was made, there's no forgiving to do for this specific part of the debt. Cross it off the list because it's been paid for.

> *(2) He owes me a confession of what he did.*
> *(2) ~~He needs to pay for the therapy I'm in trying to deal with all this.~~   P*
> *(2) He needs to pay for the doctor's visit to examine my black eye.*

Note: You will use Worksheet 3 for Steps Three and Four as well.

Chapter Four

| State the wrong done | State the debt owed | Who will be the debt collector | Mark the debt "PAID IN FULL" | Absorb the damage | Treat them as forgiven |

Who Will be the Debt Collector

The court determined a wrong was done against you and it's been documented.

The court determined the debt the offending person owes you and it's been documented.

This is where all those statements such as "let it go" … "let go and let God" … etc. come into play. But there's more to it than that.

Now comes the question you have to answer, "Who will be the one in charge of collecting this debt?"

It's your turn to act. It's for you to name the debt collector. Here's where your personal philosophy comes into play. Who or what, are your options? You really only have two options as to who or what will be responsible for collecting on this debt the court documented as legitimate.

This is Step Three.

Debt Collectors

1. *Yourself*

The first person you can name to be responsible for collecting on this debt is yourself. You were the one wronged, the debt is owed to you so you can keep the debt list the court hands out and attempt to collect on it yourself.

You can try to right the wrong on your own. The problem with you trying to collect on the debt yourself is—because you're so close to the wrong, the debt and the pain—it will be easy for you to either over or under collect.

If you over-collect—extract more from the offending person than the debt list actually states—you've just wronged that person and now you owe them. You're still connected to the person and the wrong and the pain goes around and around and you're never free.

If you under-collect—you don't collect what really is owed and the offending person does in fact "get off the hook" with this debt—the full debt has not been collected on and you're not free from the other person or the pain. You can't move on.

The bigger issue is, either way, you'll still be connected to the person, the pain and for who knows how long. Back to the suitcase word picture, you'll be carrying this suitcase for some time before you can—if ever—be free from it. Is that what you really want?

It's still an option.

There's a chance you will be able to collect exactly what is owed to you. It won't make it like it never happened but the debt will be paid. Then you can move on.

There's a perception that if you hold onto the debt list yourself it will be a reminder to you so you never get hurt that way again. It's hard to admit you actually got hurt, you fell for that, you were actually tricked, and keeping the debt list—whether you try to collect on it or not—*will ensure* you never get hurt that way again. Maybe, maybe not.

It's your choice, but I would suggest there are better ways to learn and remember how to keep yourself safe without having to carry this suitcase around for the rest of your life. The real experience you've been through can be enough of a "reminder" and a "lesson learned" without lugging the suitcase around everywhere you go.

Think it over and see if you can find an easier—and healthier—way to remember. Then consider transferring the debt collecting job over to *Other* to make life a bit easier for you.

2. *Other*

I use the word *Other* to cover a wide range of philosophies. You may hold to a belief that states, "What goes around comes around", or Karma, or any similar perspective. Any philosophy that believes there's a something or someone—outside of you—that will right the wrongs someway, somehow, some time. Whether your philosophy has a "higher power" or a higher force or essence, you hold to a belief that a something or someone outside yourself will—in time—right the wrong.

It's under this category of *Other* where I place God as well. Why? Because God is an *Other.* God is outside of you.

If God is a just and holy God—which I believe He is—then wrongs must be righted. And this particular wrong done against you will be made right and the debt will be collected on, someplace, sometime, by God.

This may be a good time to quote the Bible on God's debt collecting promise, "Do not take vengeance, my friends, but leave room for God's wrath, for it is written: 'It is mine to avenge; I will repay,' says the Lord." [1]

Doubts and Questions

If you consider the *Other* option, this step can challenge your belief system to its core. Will the wrongs *really* get righted by what, or whom, I believe in? Will what goes around *really* come back around? Will God *really* justify this wrong? Does God even *care*? What if I've messed up and I deserve this? Will good *really* win out over evil? Does this wrong even matter in ideals, or to a higher power or God out there?

62

Are any of these questions bouncing around in your mind as you read this?

Remember the pain and woundedness behind the wrongs that have been done. If you're going to hand over the responsibility of collecting on the wrong that injured you, how will that something, God, ideal, belief, *actually* manage this debt? If you're like most human beings you're not willing to give something this deep and this costly to something or someone you aren't sure will, or can, handle it correctly. Will the wrong actually—for real—be righted?

Step Three may take weeks, months, maybe even years to achieve clarity in what or who it is you're going to pass this debt document on to, because it *is* very important to you. And rightly so. Forgiving *is* for real. The steps are real with real intensions behind each and every step so your choice of whom/what is going to be the debt collector has to be real and confirmed in your own heart and mind. We're back on, "heart time", and this step in the journey will take as long as it takes. Please don't attempt to hurry this step for your own journey or somebody else's. It's too important; it's too deep and personal.

Time to Choose

When you're ready; if you chose to name *Yourself* as the debt collector, keep the list and store it somewhere. You can skip Chapters Five and Six if you want and pick up your reading at Chapter Seven. The next steps of forgiving are not for you then. Like I stated earlier, you'll remain connected to the debt list which keeps you connected to the hurt and pain until you completely collect the debt.

If you're open to the *Other* option, I encourage you to read Chapters Five and Six and keep your mind open.
When you're ready; if you chose to give the debt collecting responsibility over to *Other*, take the debt list document(s) you've written out and symbolically give it away; physically "let it go." Whatever you need to do to help you solidify in your heart and mind that you're giving the responsibility for collecting this debt—these debts—to *Other*, do so.

What I often do with clients, once they transfer the court document(s) over to **Other**, is to take those papers and make or name them "copies" of the original court documents the client just "let go" of. You'll see why in Chapter Five.

The transfer has been made.

You forgave the offending person their wrong against you.

The gavel drops.

Court is adjourned and the case is closed.

You forgave the offending person.

This leads us to Step Four described in Chapter Five.

Angie

This step, determining the debt collector, took Angie a long time to process through. She knew all the right responses. She knew she's commanded to forgive. But is this God even *real*? Does this God even *care* about her? What if God just "washes it all away"? What will Angie chose to believe for herself, not because she was told to or because her parents do? What does *Angie* really believe in?

As you can imagine, working through all these questions took time. In actual therapy session-time, this step took the longest to complete.

Finally, Angie chose to transfer the debt collecting duties over to **Other,** the God she now believed in and trusted in for herself.

Workbook Session

State the wrong done | State the debt owed | Who will be the debt collector | Mark the debt "PAID IN FULL" | Absorb the damage | Treat them as forgiven

Step 3 – Who will be the Debt Collector?

Use Worksheet 3 again

There are two options to choose between when it comes to deciding who will manage the debt collecting task:

Yourself
Other

If you choose to keep the debt list and collect on it yourself, what's your plan? How will you know if/when the debt has been paid completely?

_____

_____

_____

_____

_____

_____

_____

Enter the date you name yourself as debt collector:

_____

Head and Heart Check:

Is your reason for keeping the debt list to actually collect what they owe you, or is it because you want revenge? What are your intensions behind keeping the list yourself?

_____
_____
_____
_____
_____
_____
_____
_____

Do you have an *Other* you trust? If so, identify what or who *Other* is. It's important you understand this *Other* and why you trust this *Other* enough to transfer the debt collecting duties. You need to be sure of *Other* or you won't completely let go of the debt list. As stated in this chapter, this step may be the one that takes the longest for you to sort through and complete. This step is worth the time and effort to do well because the forgiving journey is that important.

_____
_____
_____
_____
_____
_____

If you're ready to give the list over to *Other*, do so and write down the date to remind yourself you took this step.

_____

_____

_____

_____

_____

_____

_____

_____

If you're not ready—yet—to give the debt list over to *Other*, what questions do you need answered before you can make the decision to transfer the debt collecting task to *Other*?

_____

_____

_____

_____

_____

_____

_____

_____

_____

Chapter Five

State the wrong done | State the debt owed | Who will be the debt collector | Mark the debt "PAID IN FULL" | Absorb the damage | Treat them as forgiven

Paid in Full

The court determined a wrong was done against you and it's been documented.

The court determined the debt the offending person owes you and it's been documented.

You chose **Other** to be responsible for collecting on the debt.

Here's where those papers you just "let go" of become "copies" of the actual court documents. Take your "copy" and mark "PAID IN FULL" across each page because as far as you are concerned they are. That's what you did by transferring the collecting duties to **Other**. The offending person doesn't "owe" you anymore. **Other** is collecting the debt. You forgive them and release the debt they owe you.

But why the copies? Because they prove …

It *did* happen …

It *was* wrong …

There *is* a debt …

It *will* be collected on …

68

That's forever true and real.

This is important to remember. The wrong and the debt don't just disappear when you forgive. No. They don't get forgotten by God, either. They're recorded in heaven *forever* and they *will* be collected on … just not by you.

If you want to keep your copy of the debt lists of what's owed to you as a reminder, do so. If you need to keep it to remind yourself when and where you transferred the debt collecting duties over to **Other**, do so.

Or you may want to take your copy and burn it, tear it up, take it to your church, leave it at the altar or give it to the priest or whatever is your church's tradition. Again, do what you need to do to help you physically and symbolically transfer the debt collecting responsibility from yourself to **Other**.

Now you're not connected to the debt list anymore …

Which means you're not connected to the wrong anymore …

Which means you just stepped away from the pain and woundedness …

And the offending person …

And you are free to heal.

Notice I said, "free to heal." Just because you, "let go", of the debt collecting duty doesn't mean all is fine and well and wonderful. Yes, this is a huge step, the crux step, but the pain will still take time—"heart time"—to heal.

You may still have lots of physical, emotional, mental and/or spiritual healing to do. You may still have lots of anger toward the offending person. You may still have lots of anxiety that it might happen to you again. You may still have lots of confusion and conflicting emotions. All of this is normal.

But now, you're finally free to heal.

Angie

Angie chose to take the Wrong lists (remember, there were two people who wronged her) and the debt list, and shred them into small pieces over my waste bracket. I was her official "witness" of this step. If she ever needed to be reminded whether the wrongs actually happened, that they were really wrong, that both her parents owed her a debt she chose to let her *Other* (God) to collect, all she had to do was call me or remember this particular therapy session.

What About the Debt?

> "What happens to the debt and the collecting action now?"

That's a great question without any simple answers. I'll try my best to be as clear as I can. So much of the answer to your question depends on what or who *Other* is to you.

If your *Other* is a belief, force, sense or creed that adheres to some form of ultimate justice ... you wait. It will come around sometime, somewhere and someway. The hard part is waiting, and waiting, and waiting some more. And when it does come back around and the wrong gets righted, you may or may not see it. Often we want to be there to see it and that's normal. Sometimes that does happen, sometimes it doesn't. Hold on, justice will prevail.

If your *Other* is God, a higher power or spiritual being ... you wait. God will right the wrong sometime, somewhere and someway. And the waiting is still hard. And when the wrong gets righted, you may or may not see it. So, you hold on too, justice will prevail.

If your *Other* is God, there's the personal dimension too. God does care what happened to you. He cares about you. He will not forget. And He's invested in your healing even more than you are.

Either way, you remember; you hold on to the belief that the debt will get collected on and the wrongs will be righted in the end.

You wait.

And you heal.

And you go on with your life.

And you go on to Step Five.

Workbook Session

State the wrong done	State the debt owed	Who will be the debt collector	Mark the debt "PAID IN FULL"	Absorb the damage	Treat them as forgiven

Step Four – Paid in Full

Use Worksheet 3 again

If you gave the debt collecting job over to **_Other_**, take your Worksheet 3 and mark PAID IN FULL in big bold letters across the entire page (or pages). What emotions arise as you complete this step?

_____

_____

_____

_____

_____

_____

_____

_____

_____

_____

You transferred the debt and the debt collecting duty over to **_Other_**. The person who wronged you doesn't owe you anything anymore. Sometimes this is hard to remember; that's the reason you're encouraged to write down the date. If you need to keep Worksheet 3 as a reminder, do so. Put it in a safe and private place.

Make a note where you placed that list.

_____

_____

_____

_____

If you don't need to keep your Worksheet 3, decide how you will destroy the debt list and do so. Is it enough to throw the list in the trash or do you need something more symbolic like burning it, shredding it into tiny pieces over a trash can? Think through what will best help you experience the sense of "letting it go."

Chapter Six

State the wrong done | State the debt owed | Who will be the debt collector | Mark the debt "PAID IN FULL" | Absorb the damage | Treat them as forgiven

Absorbing the Damage

The court determined a wrong was done against you and it's been documented.

The court determined the debt the offending person owes you and it's been documented.

You chose *Other* to be responsible for collecting the debt.

Your copy of the documents is marked "PAID IN FULL."

The gavel drops.

Court is adjourned.

So what happens now? I mean, once the proceedings end and you walk out of the courtroom is everything all better?

"I don't think so."

I don't think so either.

The act of forgiving isn't complete ... yet. Yes, the court part is done, but there's still more to forgiving. Let's keep going.

Step Five – You suffer; you absorb the damage yourself.

As you leave court, you absorb the damage done to you. You choose to do whatever you need to do to heal. This isn't all that new or different. You're already suffering the hurt, pain and damage from the offense. This is what you're healing from. But this isn't the, "suffering the damage", I'm talking about in this step. With Step Five comes *additional* damages—cost is probably an easier word to use to make sense here—you take on. Let me use a word picture in which you damaged my car to make this idea of, "suffering" or "absorbing the damage," understandable.

Say you got mad at me, found my car in the parking lot and broke out my windshield. The forgiving steps are easy to identify in this example:

Step One – Breaking my windshield is wrong.

Step Two – You owe me a new windshield.

Step Three – I gave **Other** the debt list.

Step Four – My copy is marked "PAID IN FULL."

The gavel drops.

Court is adjourned.

Okay, great so far.

I walk out of the courtroom and did someone or something magically fix my windshield?

"Are you out of your mind?"

My point exactly.

So what about my windshield? What happens now? How does my windshield get fixed? Who *absorbs* the cost of fixing my windshield?

This is Step Five, which is still part of forgiving. *I* take my car and have someone fix my windshield. *I* pay the cost. *I* suffer. I already suffered the hurt and damages from you breaking out my windshield in the first place.

Now ... *I* absorb the cost of installing a new windshield. *I* pay for it out of *my* own pocket.

I suffer the lost wages for the time *I* spend getting a new windshield installed.

I absorb the cost.

I suffer the damage.

You hear it?

"But, that's not fair!"

You're so right. But forgiving isn't about fair, it's about disconnecting so you can heal and move on freely with your life.

So, I absorb the damages. I do what I have to do in order to heal—fix my car—and move on. And that, "doing what I have to do to move on", cost me. Sometimes the cost comes in the form of something physical, financial, emotional, or any number of other ways.

It costs to heal. And I absorb—suffer—the cost of healing. I don't accept the *blame* or absorb the *fault*. This is a hugely important differentiation to make.

This is Step Five.

Absorb What?

Absorbing the cost of a new windshield for my car is easy to comprehend because it's tangible. But there are so many things in life that happen that aren't tangible. What if you were raped? What cost do you absorb then?

76

Here's a list—I'm sure it's not everything—of some of the things you may suffer when you let go of the hurt and pain:

> Any physical injury you received and the medical costs to care for those injuries.

> Any emotional damage you received and the cost of time, energy and services it takes to get over the PTSD, panic attacks, anger, shame, depression, anxiety, phobias or whatever came about because of being raped.

> It may mean you choose to geographically relocate; and all the costs that entails in so many different ways.

> It may mean you choose—or have—to get another job; and all the time, hassles and costs it takes to find and secure another job.

Not a small list is it? Not at all.

> "But my situation is so-n-so at work lied about me to the management and it cost me that promotion I was counting on. What do I suffer?"

Here's a list I can come up with for you:

> Lost wages because you didn't get a pay increase and any other perks that came with that new position.

> You take a "ding" to your reputation and your resume; again, unfair.

> Lost the "toys" you were thinking about purchasing with the raise that didn't come.

> Pain to your personal and/or professional confidence.

These are a few things you will absorb as you let go of the wrong done against you.

And if you were physically and/or sexually abused as a child at the hands of a step-father, what do you absorb—suffer—then?

This list will by no means be complete, but hopefully it will give you a good starting point:

> Any physical injury you received as a child and the medical costs to care for those injuries now as an adult. Yes, some injuries don't get proper medical attention until years later.

> You live with, and have to compensate for, any permanent physical injuries and/or disabilities because of their abuse.

> Maybe you can't have children of your own.

> Maybe you have to adjust to living with brain damage and all the ramifications, limitations and pain associated with traumatic brain injuries.

> Any emotional damage you received and the cost of time, energy and services it takes to get over the PTSD, panic attacks, anger, shame, depression, anxiety or phobias that you can finally address and get healing from.

> The fallout of any number of broken and/or dysfunctional relationships and the mental, relational, emotional anguish from those relationships.

> Being without "family" during the holidays.

> Having to protect your own children from the grandparent.

> The cost of legally changing your name to distance yourself even further from the perpetrator.
> Dealing with the confusion and anger at God.

Each of us will have a different list of things we absorb when it comes to doing what we need to do so we can disconnect, heal and move on with our lives.

This is exactly why forgiving is *never* cheap, quick or easy.

Resentment

> "I'm having a real hard time with this, it's not fair or right."

Exactly. So let me take the broken windshield example in a different direction. Say I choose *not* to "absorb the damage." Say I decide to drive all around town with a broken windshield. When people ask me why I'm driving around with a damaged windshield, I tell them, "Oh, you see, so-n-so broke my windshield, but I forgave them and that's why I don't have a repaired windshield." How mature of me.

> "Don't kid yourself."

Did I "let go" of the debt?

> "Yes."

Did I "let go" of the hurt and pain for real?

> "No."

Right. Hear the difference?

Have *I* done what *I* need to do in order to *move on* with my life?

> "Not really."

Exactly. This is resentment. Resentment is when you refuse to let go of the pain, hurt or injury done to you. Maybe you let go of the debt, but you're still hanging on tight to the pain and damage. And who do you damage when you refuse to pay up or absorb the cost and take the action necessary to heal and move on?

> "Myself?"

Exactly. Is that what you want?

This is not a rhetorical question; it's a real one. There are people who choose to hold on to the hurt and become resentful. As clinicians, we say they're "playing the victim", or the "woe is me

…" attitude. The, "I'm hurt and helpless. I need you to come and rescue me", assuming a victim mentality.

Go ahead and drive through life without a windshield and see where that gets you. Who are you hurting? Is the person that broke your windshield absorbing any cost? Again, it's a choice you face and have to make. It's the same as choosing your position when you take up residency in the hospital. It's being a victim rather than being victimized.

> "Why would anybody keep being a victim?"

Some people are too wounded to be able to do anything to remedy their situation. Some don't know what to do. Still others realize there's a lot of power in being "powerless." Call it enabling, victim-stance, passive-aggressive, or whatever. Intentional or not, conscious or not, holding on to the hurt, pain and injury is a very powerful manipulation ploy people use as they attempt to control others for their own benefit. Again, not a part of our focus here, so I'll move on.

If you choose to hold on to the hurt, pain and damage the offending person did to you, you'll shut down right here, right now. You won't move on, you won't heal and you won't complete your forgiving journey. You'll be stuck.

And you won't feel the freedom that awaits you at the end of the journey.

This option isn't easy, it just has a better outcome. To forgive means to let go of the pain and absorb the damages—the cost—it takes to heal and move on in life.

> "No way. That's way too much to absorb. I can't—I won't—do that."

That's your choice. I'll be straight with you; what are your options? Think about them:

> Option one: You keep the hurt and don't let go. You become resentful and sit down in the middle of the pain and brokenness and carry another suitcase around, drive

around with a broken windshield and never heal or become free. Sounds like lots and lots of pain, misery and discomfort to me and you're only doing (more) damage to yourself. You become a victim rather than being a person who's been victimized.

Option two: You let go of the hurt and pain so you can move on. You've been victimized, but you refuse to become a victim. Again, it's not fair. It's Step Five.

And Choose. Choose "hard place" (option two) and let go. This option has a better ending.

Angie

So what damage did Angie absorb?

She lived with the pain of a black and swollen eye for a couple of weeks. She fielded all the questions from friends and adults as to how she got the black eye. She chose to attend therapy, which cost her time and energy. She chose to face the pain, the disappointment, the loss of having a real father. She chose to deal with her anger toward her father and her mother. She chose to wrestle with the *why* questions and all the confusion those questions bring. She chose to suffer the damages.

Fortunately, she didn't have to pay for her own therapy too. Had she been an adult on her own, she would have paid my therapy bill out of her own pocket.

Again, was it hard?

You bet it was.

Did it take time and energy away from other things Angie could have been doing as a teen?

For sure.

She chose.

She chose to absorb the damages so she could be free and move on.

This absorbing the damage is part of forgiving. Not absorbing the damage means you didn't forgive ... you didn't finish the journey.

Another Chance

> "Yeah, okay, I'm resentful and have been for a long time. I never let go of the hurt and pain so-n-so caused me. So what do I do now? Am I damned to be stuck here forever?"

You're never damned. It doesn't matter how long you've been shut down here, you can choose—now—to get up and finish forgiving that person.

It's not too late.

It's never too late to get up ...

And pay up.

To let go of the pain.

Absorb the damages.

And move on.

It is fair?

No.

Is it supposed to be this way? You get left with paying to "fix" something in your life you didn't break?

No.

It's still the next step in finishing your forgiving journey.

Remembering the Pain

When you remember the "good ole days" you often feel the warm, fuzzy feelings that are associated with those positive and happy memories.

When you remember the "bad ole days" don't be surprised if you feel the ache, anger, disgust, sadness and/or pain that are associated with those negative memories.

> "What's the difference between that and being resentful?"

That's a huge question.

If you're resentful, you never let go of the hurt and pain. It's always right here. It might look to others as if you're wearing a heavy, ragged old coat that's weighing you down. You may be living the "Oh, poor me" victim mentality, consciously or not. Anger can probably be found just under the surface of your everyday normal demeanor, it's present. You're still driving around with a busted windshield. The windshield is still damaged, you still have pain. It's now; it's here. That's being resentful.

If you forgave and absorbed the damage and moved on, you were simply reminded of the offense; something triggered it *back* into your memory. It wasn't now; it wasn't here until something brought it *back* to mind.

Make sense?

It's important to know that if it took something to cause you to remember the event, the offense, or that person again for the feelings to come back, it's not resentment. That's normal.

It's important to know too that just because you remember the offense doesn't mean you didn't forgive in full. Remember the story of Joseph.

It's important to know that just because you still hurt and are wounded doesn't mean you didn't forgive in full. Remember, healing takes "heart time" and can't be hurried.

It's important to know that just because you think of the offense occasionally, doesn't automatically mean you have "unfinished business" of some kind. Remembering the "bad" days can bring back the "bad" emotions, that's all.

Workbook Session

State the wrong done | State the debt owed | Who will be the debt collector | Mark the debt "PAID IN FULL" | Absorb the damage | Treat them as forgiven

Step 5 – Absorbing the Damage

Use Worksheet 4

For each wrong you listed on Worksheet 2, write out the damages you suffered, or are suffering. As you do, think about the tangible—as well as any intangible—damages the wrong created.

Angie:

(2) I have to physically heal and hope my eye isn't permanently damaged.

(2) I have to answer all the question on how I got my black eye.

(2) I have to go to therapy to get my life—that he screwed up—back together as best I can.

(2) I have to live with the fact that I don't have a real father in my life.

As you work on Worksheet 4 what emotions come up for you?

_____

_____

_____

_____

_____

_____

_____

Once your list is complete, decide which damages can be healed and mark each with an **H** (heal-able). If its damage that will always be with you and never completely go away—permanent—mark it with an **F** (forever).

If you've already healed from the damage that is heal-able, circle the **H** to indicate it's healed.

Angie:

---

(2) I have to physically heal and hope my eye isn't permanently damaged.   H

(2) I have to answer all the questions on how I got my black eye.   H

(2) I have to go to therapy to get my life—that he screwed up—back together as best I can.   H

(2) I have to live with the fact that I don't have a real father in my life.   F

As you look over the damages you marked with an **F** (forever) what thoughts and emotions do you have?

_____

_____

_____

_____

_____

_____

_____

_____

_____

_____

_____

_____

_____

_____

_____

_____

_____

_____

_____

_____

_____

_____

Chapter Seven

State the wrong done   State the debt owed   Who will be the debt collector   Mark the debt "PAID IN FULL"   Absorb the damage   Treat them as forgiven

Treating Them as Forgiven

The court determined a wrong was done against you and it's been documented.

The court determined the debt the offending person owes you and it's been documented.

You chose *Other* to be responsible for collecting on the debt.

Your copy of the documents is marked "PAID IN FULL."

The gavel drops.

Court is adjourned.

You absorbed the damage so you could move on.

The final step in the forgiving journey is to treat that offending person as forgiven … because they are. You treat them as if they don't owe you anything … because they don't.

The forgiving journey is complete; it ends here.

But …

This is exactly where all sorts of *relationship* topics get tossed in—incorrectly—and make the action of forgiving so confusing, convoluted and more than it actually is. People try to make forgiving the "fix" for the relationship too.

The relationship may not be fixed. This is true, this is real.

Treating them as forgiven does *not* mean you trust them.

Treating them as forgiven does *not* mean things are reconciled between the two of you.

Treating them as forgiven does *not* mean it never happened.

Treating them as forgiven does *not* mean you must interact with the person in a friendly manner—or interact with them at all ever again.

Keep it simple. Treating them as forgiven *only* means you don't bring up the wrong committed or the debt incurred. You remember, you may still be healing, but you don't bring it up to them. You don't "throw it in their face", as we say, overtly or covertly.

That's all.

They don't owe you anything anymore. They *still* have to pay the debt, just not to you. You don't look to them to pay it back or "make things right" or anything.

They don't owe you a new windshield.

They don't owe you an apology.

They don't owe you the money they stole from you.

They don't owe you a "thank you for forgiving me" (assuming the debt "disappeared", which you and I know is not the truth; it just changed hands).

You forgave them, now *you live* out that forgiving.

> "Easier said than done."

True.

Angie

Angie did just that. She never talked about the black eye fight with her father. She still didn't trust him (more on this in Chapter Ten). She didn't trust her mother to protect her if the need ever arose again, either. The relationships weren't "fixed" but Angie was able to disconnect, heal and move on with her life.

Guarded

> "So what do I do now, because I live with the person who wronged me; I see them every day?"

You do the same thing Angie did. You don't talk about this past wrong to the offender.

That's it.

Yes, it can be much harder when that person's presence reminds you of the wrong—a lot harder. Still, it's a topic you don't bring up.

That's Step Six. That's all treating the person as forgiven means. Nothing more than that.

Remember, forgiving takes place in a court of law; it's a legal-type of transaction. It has nothing to do with emotions, opinions, perceptions or relating to another person.

So ... the relating that goes on between the two of you will be strained. It will be awkward and you will be guarded. Let me say it again, forgiving is not designed to address or fix the relationship between the two of you. The relationship issue is what Part II is all about.

Workbook Session

| State the wrong done | State the debt owed | Who will be the debt collector | Mark the debt "PAID IN FULL" | Absorb the damage | Treat them as forgiven |

Step 6 – Treating them as Forgiven

What will be the hardest part for you in *"treating them as forgiven"*? Why?

_____

_____

_____

_____

_____

_____

What steps can you take to make it easier for yourself?

_____

_____

_____

_____

_____

_____

Remember, treating them as forgiven doesn't mean you trust them or things are "all better" now. It only means you don't remind the person of the wrong done ever again.

As you've worked the steps described you can be sure you forgave for real! You have the "court" documents to prove it too. There may still be a lot of healing you need to do, you may still feel a lot of pain and/or sorrow, all that's normal. Just getting to the place where you forgave the person(s) is a *huge* step in your healing journey. Be patient and give yourself the time you need to heal, even if it takes longer than you'd like.

Take some time to journal what this journey has been like for you to this point. There's more to do in this process and book, however, it's still important to write out your thoughts and emotions you have experienced upon reaching this key place.

_____

_____

_____

_____

_____

_____

_____

_____

_____

_____

_____

_____

_____

PART II

The chapters in Part II could be stand-alone mini-books because they're separate topics altogether from the topic of forgiving. The reason I'm including them here is because these are the topics that often get thrown into the blender with forgiving in an attempt to make the relationship part, "all better" and "fixed."

It will be important to remember as you read the following chapters that they pick up *after* the court of law legal-type transaction is completed. All these topics address the *relational* aspects of the situation that got strained or totally destroyed because of the wrong that was done against you.

I originally thought of starting Part II discussing trusting and being trustworthy. That's usually the topic that most frequently gets blended in with forgiving. It's also the topic that creates the most confusion and holds the most misconceptions, especially in religious contexts.

As I researched all these topics separately—which was a lot like sticking my hand into the blended ingredients and pulling each part out piece by piece—I discovered there's an actual sequence these topics follow to get to healthy trusting relationship. Here's that sequence:

- You can't trust (in a healthy way) the offending person until the two of you are reconciled.
- You can't be reconciled until you (in some form or fashion) have confronted the offending person.

So, we reverse the order and the sequence is:

Forgive (Part I)

Confront

Reconcile

Trust.

With that said, here we go.

Chapter Eight

Confronting

The topic of confronting is always close by when we talk about the need to forgive.

"Why?"

For several reasons. In normal situations (and I use the word "normal" intentionally here because there are many "not-normal" situations we'll address shortly) the way to address a wrong, forgive, heal and mend the relational tension is for the offended person to talk to the offending person. It would go something like this:

You identify and both agree on the wrong done.

You both determine and agree on the debt that's to be paid.

The offending person pays you (the offended person) the debt they owe you.

The offending person gives you a heart-felt apology.

The lesson is learned and there's a commitment to not repeat that offense.

You absorb the intangible parts of the damage the wrong caused.

The issue has been settled.

This opens up the *possibility* (not a guarantee) for the relationship to be mended.

All this took place because it began with a confrontation—a face-to-face interaction.

What Confronting is for Real

What does it mean to confront the person who wronged you? And how do you do that, for real?

---

confront \ kon **frunt** \ *(1) to approach a situation in a direct manner;*
(2) to directly challenge a person or situation regarding something; (3) to deal with something or someone in a truthful manner.

So, under normal circumstances, you approach the person who wronged you directly and in a truthful manner, with the end goal of righting the wrong and resolving the relational tension.

> "Okay, but why confront in the first place? I mean, the wrong's been done, you can't change what's already happened, so you just need to move on. Isn't that what you've been saying all along ... move on?"

If forgiving is for your (the offended person's) benefit, not the benefit of the offended person, then confronting is for whose benefit?

Great question. Here's a look.

Why Confront?

Confronting is for the offended person's benefit—but it's just as much for the *offending person's* benefit … if not more so.

Follow me on this. If all goes according to the normal interaction outlined above …

> The offending person is made aware of the wrong done and how it impacted you; they're corrected (they benefit).

>> That person is given a challenge not to do it again (they benefit).

>>> They learned from their mistake (they benefit).

>>> You get what's due you (you benefit).

>>> And hopefully they won't repeat the wrong (you both benefit).

That's how it goes in a heathy, normal interaction.

> "That's never going to happen with my ex-wife. We can't sit down and discuss anything without it turning into a fight and a blame game. She doesn't even see what she did was wrong."

That's the main reason for confronting, so the offending person can see where *they* were wrong—the actual wrong done, the law that was broken—and how it hurt you. It's to help *them* see *their* blind spot, the wrong that was done. It's to help *them* become aware of the thing they aren't aware of. Confrontation is for the benefit of the *offending person*.

Whether they see it as for their benefit, I can't guarantee.

There are therapists, clergy and well-meaning people who think the offended person *has* to confront the abuser in order to gain a sense of power and control over their own life again or to help the offended person to feel vindicated somehow. The rationale behind this viewpoint is that you (the offended person) will stay in a victim position unless you confront.

> "Didn't we address the victim position back in Step Five?"

Yes, we did.

> "I thought so."

Be careful. This approach will be beneficial *some of the time*. It can also make things worse for you (the offended person). Stay with me.

Confronting is to assist the offending person to get on the right path again, or for the first time. Confronting is *not* designed to make the offended person feel better. From the theological perspective the "normal" protocol when a wrong is done is, "If your brother sins (does wrong) against you, go and show him his fault. If he listens to you (situation stated at the beginning of this Chapter), you have won your brother over." [1] I agree and this *is* the correct way to handle a wrong done against you ...

When it's a "normal" situation ...

But ...

What if your situation is *not* normal? What if the person isn't *safe*—physically, emotionally, spiritually—for you to be close to in any capacity? What if you don't know where they live, or even if they're alive? What if that offending person is *still* (actually) out to get—re-offend—you? What do you do then?

> "Well, you still have to confront because that's what the Bible says."

Wait a minute, what about where it says, "Whoever corrects (confronts) a mocker invites insults; whoever rebukes (confronts) a wicked man incurs abuse. *Do not rebuke* (confront) a mocker or he will hate you ..." [2] (italics and parenthesis added)?

"Ummmmm."

Contra-Indications

Listen to a commercial about a prescription medication for some ailment. The advertisement says, "If you have *this* problem ... take *this* medicine and it will make you better," or some variation of that. That's the "normal" thing to do in a "normal" situation. That's the "normal" medication to take if you have *this* "normal" problem. Listen too, to the fast-paced voice at the end of the commercial. It will say something like, "*Do not* take this medication if you have high blood pressure (*this* situation) or are on blood pressure medication (*this* situation). *Do not* take this medicine if you're pregnant (*this* situation) or think you may be pregnant (*this* situation). *Do not* take if you weigh less than 130 pounds (*this* situation). *Do not* give this medication to children under the age of five (*this* situation).

Hear it?

One size does *not* fit all, especially with prescription medications and confronting.

Yes, you can take *this* medication under "normal" circumstances, but—and this is a huge "but" when it comes to medications—*do not* take this medication under *these* ("not normal") circumstances or situations. These are called contra-indications.

So it is with confronting. If you're in a "normal" situation, then go to the person one on one and confront them and see if the two of you can make amends (like those stated at the beginning of this Chapter).

But (again) ...

There are so many times when it comes to the issues we're talking about that the person and/or circumstance is *not* anywhere close to "normal." The offending person *is* dangerous, arrogant or evil. It's *not* safe for you to go and confront the offending person. You need to find an *alternative* way to deal with your situation other than confronting.

What is Safe?

Is the person a safe person?

This is the first question you have to answer before even considering whether to confront the offending person or not. How can you determine whether that offending person is a safe person or not? Once again, this is not a rhetorical question. How do you know? For real?

Too much is on the line to guess—or hope—they're safe. So, how do you know?

Ask these questions for starters:

> Was the wrong done against you accidental or intentional?

If it was accidental, have you seen clear action steps on the offending person's part—over a period of time—to keep it from happening again?

If it was intentional, have you seen a clear behavior change in the offending person's actions and attitudes that—over a period of time—show, in real terms, they won't intentionally try to wrong you again?

> Is there a history of the offending person hurting other people in the same manner?
>
> Are they honest? Is telling the truth a characteristic of their lifestyle?
>
> Is treating people with respect a characteristic of their lifestyle?
>
> Would you entrust your child into their keeping?
>
> Would you entrust something very valuable into their keeping?
>
> > "I'm not sure."

There's your answer, right there. You just told me you don't believe they're completely safe.

Because, being safe sometimes …

But sometimes not …

And sometimes …

But sometimes not …

Equals being unsafe all the time. You never know when it's safe and when it's not. That's unsafe *all* the time.

"But I believe people to be safe until they give me a reason to think differently."

Oh really? To be blunt, are you trying to sound tolerant, or generous, or what? Tell me you'd entrust your three-year old daughter to the 56 year old divorced man who just moved in down the street? Would you?

For your daughter's sake, I sure hope not. You don't know him—you don't know if he's trustworthy or not … for real.

Would you give that same man your house keys, social security number and credit card? Would you? Do you trust him that much?

According to your belief, he hasn't done anything to show you he's "not safe." So, you'll believe he *is* safe until he gives you reason *not* to believe that?

If you really believe that, it could be too late, because he may have harmed your daughter, robbed you or stolen your identity. Oops, now he's proved himself to be an unsafe person …

But it's too late for you and your daughter! The wrongs have been done.

It will be too late because his "giving you a reason to think differently (that he's not safe)" as you say, will have cost you your daughter's safety, your electronics, bank accounts and identity because those will have been stolen. Oops, now he's proved himself to be an unsafe person …

There are lots and lots of people who are *not* safe and you *can't* tell just by looking at them, talking with them or checking their job resume. More on this when we get to Chapter Ten and talk about trust and being trustworthy.

If they're *not* safe, simple, you *don't* confront. You *stay away* so they can't hurt you again.

That's the "medication" or caution you take in *these* situations—the contra-indication—because the "normal" medication of confronting is *not* the "medication" to take in situations like these.

That's it … and it's spiritual too.

SIDE NOTE: If you truly believe people to be safe until they prove to you otherwise, let me encourage you to seek out a trained mental health professional so you can look at and think over your belief system. There may need to be some changes that are important for you to consider making. I'm not diagnosing you with any disorder or assume you're dysfunctional, but consider this a strong encouragement.

When to and when not to …

Forgiving and Confronting Flow Chart

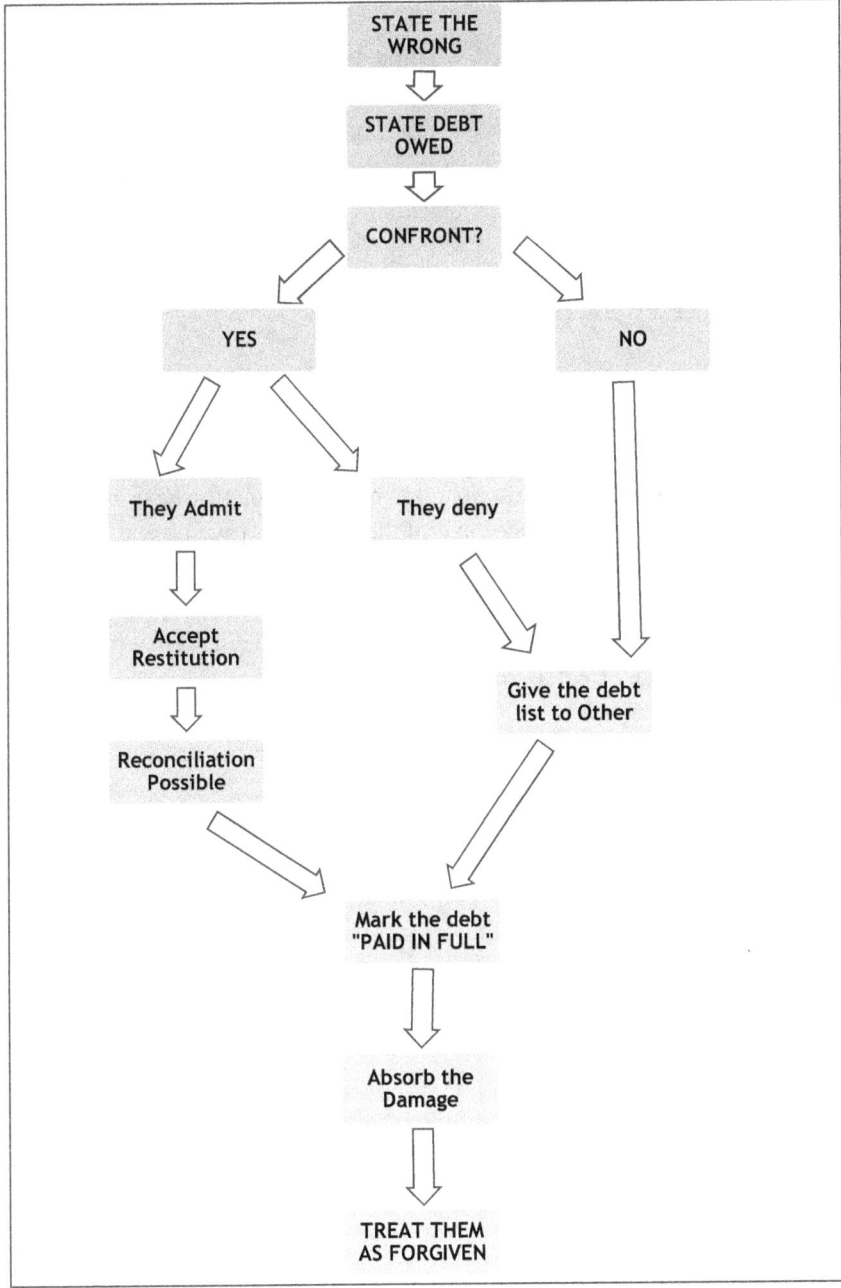

Let's work through the flow chart from start to finish. Here are the confront scenarios.

Confront and Admit – "normal or best case"

This is the "normal" situation we talked about earlier.

> 1. You determine the offending person *is* safe enough to confront and it's geographically possible to confront them.
>
> 2. You decide you're far enough along in your healing journey you can do the confronting.
>
> 3. You decide your motives are right, for their benefit, not for revenge or to attack back.
>
> 4. You confront them and show them when, where and how they wronged you and the debt they owe to you (Chapters Two and Three).
>
> 5. They confess, give a legitimate apology and pay the debt they owe to you.
>
> 6. You accept their apology. You accept the restitution of the debt.
>
> 7. You and the offending person are reconciled (more on this in Chapter Nine). This does not mean the relationship is all "fixed," just that moving forward is possible.
>
> 8. You mark the debt list "PAID IN FULL" (Chapter Five).
>
> 9. You absorb any damage/cost not covered by their restitution (Chapter Six).

10. You treat them as forgiven and don't bring it up to them anymore (Chapter Seven).

Forgiving is completed and confronting was successfully completed too. Successful because the offender confessed and paid the debt owed to you.

Confront and Deny

This starts off like the "normal" situation we talked about earlier.

1. You determine the offending person *is* safe enough to confront and it's geographically possible to confront them.

2. You decide you're far enough along in your healing journey that you can do the confronting.

3. You decide your motives are right, for their benefit, not for revenge or to attack back.

4. You confront them and show them when, where and how they wronged you and the debt they owe to you (Chapters Two and Three).

5. They deny the wrong doing and/or blame you for the wrong.

6. You accept—not agree with—the denial and leave.

7. You choose to give the debt collecting responsibility to *Other* (Chapter Four).

8. There is no reconciling (more on this in Chapter Nine).

9. You mark the debt list "PAID IN FULL" (Chapter Five).

10. You absorb the damage (Chapter Six).

11. You treat them as forgiven and don't bring it up to them anymore (Chapter Seven).

Forgiving is completed; confronting is completed too, but without a successful outcome. Unsuccessful because the offender didn't confess and didn't pay the debt owed to you.

Not Confront

This is the *not* "normal" situation—the contra-indication—we talked about.

1. You determine the offending person is *not* safe enough to confront even if it's geographically possible to confront them.

2. You choose to give the debt collecting responsibility to *Other* (Chapter Four).

3. There is no reconciling (more on this in Chapter Nine).

4. You mark the debt list "PAID IN FULL" (Chapter Five).

5. You absorb the damage (Chapter Six).

6. You treat them as forgiven and don't bring it up to them anymore (Chapter Seven).

Forgiving is completed and you move on.

Those are the three options as each one plays out. It's important to take your time and determine whether this is truly a safe person and situation to confront.

I can't stress this enough; make sure you're far enough along in your forgiving and healing journey *before* confronting. If you choose to confront and the offending person denies the wrong took place, or blames you for the wrong, it can be as traumatizing—maybe even more so—than when the wrong first happened. You can be wronged again and the hurt and pain from this wrong may be overwhelming when added to the hurt and pain you're already dealing with. Please be careful.

How to Confront

"So how do I confront in a smart and healthy way?"

Now comes the moment of truth. You confront (Step 4 in the progression listed above). Whenever possible, confront face-to-face. Skype and/or phone are acceptable if meeting in person is not possible. I would not suggest confronting by written communication: letter, email or text message.

"Why not in writing?"

For the following reasons:

1. It's impersonal and the wrong done is a personal issue between the two of you.

2. Either of you will be more prone to say things over email or texting that you would not dare say face-to-face.

3. Anything in written or electronic form can be accessed by others, even if inadvertently. The offense is between the two of you, it's personal. Don't risk having the entire world know.

Rehearse what you will say beforehand. You may want to make up an outline to follow when you confront.

Stick to the facts—the court room procedures and documents— and keep yourself as un-emotional and objective as you can when confronting to minimize emotional escalation for either you. If confronting is successful and you go on to mend the relationship, then emotional expression is appropriate.

Lay out the facts that are needed for a true apology; the who, what, when and where. Lay out the debt that is owed, the restitution needed, as well.

Your whole confronting presentation can be kept to about four or five sentences. Keep it short and to the point.

Then be quiet. Wait. Give the offending person time to process your confrontation and consider their response. Keep in mind, you've been processing the offense for some time, this confrontation may be unexpected by the offender. As hard as it may be to wait, don't hurry their response. Wait for them to either *admit* or *deny*.

Accept whatever response the person gives you. *Don't try to force an apology or admission.* Don't press them to ask for your forgiveness. This is you confronting them, not you trying to get them to do what you think they should.

Have a plan in place to end the confronting and go your way. This will be especially important if the confronting does not go well. It's a way to keep yourself safe. You may want to share with someone you trust when and where the confrontation is to be. A plan can simply be knowing what you will say to close the confronting conversation. For example, you can thank the offender for meeting with you, whether it goes well or not keep it simple and concise. Rehearse the closing.

This is a general outline of how to confront the offending person. Some situations may require a variation of this outline and that's to be expected. I can't over-emphasize the need to keep it brief, direct and factual. If you don't think you can do that then I'd suggest not confronting at this time.

Confronting Symbolically

> "My Father's been dead for over nine years now. How do I confront a person who's dead?"

108

You can't. Just like you can't confront a person face-to-face when you don't know where they are. You can however, do something symbolic in place of a face-to-face encounter. If you're someone that prefers tangible and concrete in order to help let go of the wrong, consider writing a letter (this is an exception to the earlier suggestion) to the offending person. Here's what the flow chart steps would look like in this case:

1. There is no issue of safety here.

2. You still want to make sure you're far enough along with your healing journey so this symbolic confronting won't throw you back and re-injure you.

3. You still want to make sure your motive is right but this step is not as critical as if confronting in person.

4. Here is where you actually write the letter. Use the same suggestions listed above about how to confront the offending person:

You may want to make up an outline to follow when you confront.

Stick to the facts—the court room procedures and documents—and keep yourself as objective and un-emotional as you can when writing out your confrontation.

Lay out the facts that are needed in a true apology; the who, what, when and where. Lay out the debt that is owed, the restitution that is needed, as well.

Even with a letter, your whole confronting presentation can be kept to about four or five sentences. Keep it short and to the point. If there's more you want to say to the person, write a second letter. That's where you can write all the other things you'd like to tell that person. This second letter is where emotion expression is appropriate and helpful.

5. There will be no *admitting or confession* in response to your letter. You can take this either way; they would have admitted the wrong had they been alive or you can take the obvious silence as they *deny* the wrong and/or blame you for the wrong.

6. You decide what you want to do with the letter. You can choose to keep the letter as a reminder along with the court documents you saved as a reminder that you did "confront" the offending person. You may want to destroy it somehow: rip it up, burn it or bury it somewhere. Either way, ensure it won't be seen by somebody else unless you choose to show it to them.

7. You choose to give the debt collecting responsibility to *Other* (Chapter Four).

8. No debt can be paid or restitution made (more on this in Chapter Nine).

9. You mark the debt list "PAID IN FULL" (Chapter Five).

10. You absorb the damage (Chapter Six).

11. You treat them as forgiven. Obviously you can't bring it up to them (Chapter Seven).

Forgiving is completed; the symbolic confronting is over, and you can move on.

You may also want to read the letter aloud; to yourself, your therapist, a mentor or to *Other*. There's a technique in therapy called "empty chair" where you imagine the person who wronged you sitting in an empty chair across from you. You read the letter—or you can just verbally do the symbolic confronting—to the offending person as if they were sitting in that chair. Before you smirk at this technique, it can be very powerful and very cathartic when set up correctly.

If you're working with a mental health professional, talk about the different ways you can confront the person even though that person is not physically there.

Workbook Session

Confronting

Before you read chapter 8 in FORGIVE FOR REAL, what did you think confrontation meant or was supposed to be?

_____

_____

_____

_____

_____

_____

What similarities does your thinking have with how the book defines confronting and the reason for confronting?

_____

_____

_____

_____

_____

_____

_____

_____

_____

_____

How does your thinking differ when compared to the book's definition?

_____

_____

_____

_____

_____

_____

_____

If you're thinking of confronting the person who wronged you, what is your reason for confronting that person?

_____

_____

_____

_____

_____

_____

_____

How do you think confronting will help you?

_____

_____

_____

_____

_____

_____

_____

How do you think the confronting will help the other person?

_____

_____

_____

_____

_____

_____

_____

_____

_____

_____

Is the person you're thinking of confronting truly safe enough to confront? What makes you think they're safe? What makes you think they may not be safe?

_____

_____

_____

_____

_____

If you determined the person *is* safe enough to confront, write out what you're going to say. Remember to keep it short, concise and stick to the point.

_____

_____

_____

_____

_____

_____

_____

_____

_____

_____

_____

_____

_____

_____

_____

_____

Think through when and where you want to confront this person.
Write out your plan.

_____

_____

_____

_____

_____

_____

_____

_____

_____

_____

_____

_____

_____

_____

_____

_____

_____

Look at the Flow Chart under the Chapter's sub-heading **When To and When Not To** and work through the two options on the left side of the flow chart. Do you think the person will *admit* or *deny*? What makes you think the person will respond this way?

_____

_____

_____

_____

_____

_____

_____

_____

_____

_____

_____

_____

_____

_____

_____

If they *admit*, have in mind what restitution you will ask them to provide. Write down what you will ask them to pay back before the confrontation.

_____

_____

_____

_____

_____

_____

If they *deny*, how do you think the denial will impact you?

_____

_____

_____

_____

_____

_____

What do you need to be ready to do if your confrontation is *denied?*

_____

_____

_____

_____

_____

If you decided the person's *not* safe enough to confront, what will you do now?

_____

_____

_____

_____

_____

_____

If you don't know where the person is or if they are alive anymore, you won't be able to confront them face to face. How can you confront that person in a symbolic way that will help you move forward in your healing journey?

_____

_____

_____

_____

_____

_____

_____

_____

_____

_____

_____

_____

_____

Chapter Nine

Reconciling

Confronting comes after forgiving.

Reconciling comes after confronting.

If there's no confronting, there can be no reconciling. The confrontation has to have a successful ending first. Once again, let's look at an accurate definition of the word reconcile. Getting an accurate definition is so very important to your understanding and your actions.

reconcile \ *ra kon si l \: (a) to make two things match; (b) when two parties say the same thing.*

We don't use do this much anymore, but when you "reconcile your checking account," what does that mean?

You say, "I have $5,000 in my checking account."

The bank says, "You have $5,000 in your checking account."

Your checking account is … reconciled.

Both parties—you and the bank—say the same thing.

Did you and your bank suddenly become best buddies because you're reconciled?

"No, that's stupid."

Exactly. Reconciled means "say the same thing" and that's *all*.

If there was no confronting, there is no way you and the offending person will be reconciled. If you did confront and the offending person denied the wrong doing—not saying the same thing—there is no way the two of you will be reconciled either.

Make sense?

> You say, "Father, you physically abused me from the age of five until I left the house at age 18. It was wrong and you hurt me."

> Your father says, "I abused you physically from the age of five until you left the house at age 18. It was wrong of me and I hurt you" (the apology we talked about in Chapter Three).

The two of you are reconciled.

Your stories match. You both say the same thing about the physical abuse that happened to you.

Hold on here. We didn't say *anything* about, "things are all better and wonderful now." All that happened is the offending person and the offended person (you) are reconciled—saying the same thing. It's a misconception that reconciling is restoring.

Reconciling is saying the same thing; it has nothing to do with the restoring or mending of anything.

---

restore \ ree **stor** \: (a) to rebuild or to renew; (b) to put back into original condition form or function

---

Reconciling and restoring are *not* the same thing. Don't get them confused, keep them separate. This is exactly why defining the terms clearly is so critical.

Do you understand the difference?

Yes, your father agreed—not just said the words—with you that the wrong happened.

But that doesn't make him a safe person.

It doesn't mean you're obligated to rekindle the relationship or begin a friendship with your father.

All that happened with reconciling is both parties said the same thing … they reconciled.

That's it. Nothing more.

There's nothing that says you and your father have to go to a sporting event together. There's nothing that says the two of you have to sit beside each other in church next Sunday.
You both agree on the same thing. That's it.

> "The Bible says you're to live in peace with all men. So you *are* obligated to restore the relationship."

I believe the quote you're thinking of says, "*If it is possible*, as far as it depends on you, live at peace with everyone" [1] (italics added). It's *not possible* to "live at peace" with an offending person who denies the wrong they did against you.

How can you "live at peace" with a person who denies the truth of what they did wrong against you and is lying about it even happening?

You can't. It's *not possible*.

How can you "live at peace" with the offending person who's an unsafe individual to be in contact with?

You can't. It's *not possible* to, "live at peace", with an unsafe person. Peace and a dangerous person can't co-exist.

It's just *not possible*.

You can't make the other person choose to live in peace with you either. That's what it means, "as far as it depends on you." Not all of this, "live in peace", is yours to make happen.

Don't Force

   "I want things to be reconciled, but they don't."

Okay fine. You can't force it. If you try to *make* them reconcile with you, you become a manipulator and it won't work. You're not obligated to reconcile and neither are they.

Back to the, "don't fight reality", principle we talked about earlier. If the offending person refuses to say the same thing, there's your reality. Accept it even if it's not what you want or hoped for. It may come later, but for now you are not going to be reconciled.

So, yes, reconcile if you can—which means the confronting had a successful outcome—and *if possible* (not a command) seek to restore a healthy relationship or build a healthy relationship for the first time.

You can forgive without confronting.
You can forgive without being reconciled too.

Angie

She did not confront her father; there was no reconciling. Her mother did come forward with an appropriate apology so Angie and her mother did reconcile—they said the same thing—but there was no restoring of relationship. There was no healthy relationship there to begin with.

Did Angie forgive?

"Yes."

Did Angie confront?

"No."

Was Angie and the offending persons reconciled?

"For her father, no. For her mother, yes."

Was everything fine and wonderful after that?

"I wouldn't think so."

You're absolutely right. You got it. She did forgive. She did do what she needed to do to disconnect from the wrong done against her so she could heal and move on. Even though she healed and moved on, there was lots and lots of tension in the house.

"Daha! It's not a safe place for Angie."

Right.

Not easy for a teenage girl to do. I was proud of Angie. She did it right.

While the exact words may vary, be listening to make sure all the elements are at least covered.

Workbook Session

Reconciling

Before you read Chapter 9 in the book, what did you think reconciling meant?

_____

_____

_____

_____

_____

_____

_____

_____

_____

Was your definition similar to how the book defines reconciling, *"to say the same thing"*? If not, what was different?

_____

_____

_____

_____

_____

_____

_____

How would you describe the difference between *reconcile* and *restore* to another person?

_____

_____

_____

_____

_____

_____

_____

Have you confronted the person yet? If not, you won't be ready for the reconciling section, yet.

If you confronted the person and they *denied* the wrong done, there will be no reconciling.

If you confronted the person and they *admitted* to doing the wrong, the option to reconcile is open.

Go on to Worksheet 5

Since reconcile means, *"to say the same thing,"* write out the wrong done against you using the format of a confession—apology—for each of the wrongs you listed on Worksheet 2.

Write it out this way:

Who: (Put the person's name here)

Did what: (name the wrong done here)

Against whom: (put your name here)

It was wrong and it hurt me.

Who: (put the person's name here again)

Owes: (list the debt the person owes you to make retribution as best as they can)

To whom: (put your name here again).

Write out what the other person will need to say in order to, *"say the same thing."* Write it out this way:

Who: (Put the person's name here)

Did what: (name the wrong done here)

Against whom: (put your name here)

It was wrong and it hurt you.

Who: (put the person's name here again)

Owes: (list the debt the person owes you to make retribution as best as they can)

To whom: (put your name here again).

This is what the offending person will need to say—a confession of the wrong done—in order for the two of you to be reconciled.

Has the person made that statement yet?

_____

_____

If the person did offer a confession, how did you handle the person's confession, apology?

_____

_____

_____

_____

_____

If there is no reconciling, what do you need to do now to continue the healing process?

_____

_____

_____

_____

_____

_____

_____

_____

_____

_____

_____

_____

_____

_____

_____

_____

_____

_____

_____

_____

_____

Chapter Ten

Trust and Trustworthy

Trust is probably one of the most misunderstood subjects I help clients with in my practice. As fundamental as trust is, most of us don't get it.

Trust is a core developmental issue in a person's life. The first 12 months of a baby's life is almost exclusively focused on the issue of trust in the form of, *"is my environment safe and is there somebody out there who's trustworthy or whom I can rely on (trust) to take care of me and keep me safe?"*

To forgive does *not* mean automatically trusting the person who wronged you. In fact, there's nothing in the Bible that tell us we're to trust another person. Nowhere. It's not there. It tells us to trust God. It tells us not to trust our own understanding. But it never tells us to trust another person.

> "But I thought trust was an important part of a healthy relationship between two individuals. Why didn't God talk about it?"

The answer lies in what God *does* talk a *whole lot* about. God talks a whole lot about how to *be* a *trustworthy* person.

Trustworthy for Real

So, what does trustworthy mean? Can you give me a good definition of it? How would you explain what trustworthy is to a 13 year old? How do you know if a person is trustworthy or not? Are you supposed to trust another person until they give you a reason not to? (That sounds a whole like believing a person is "safe" until they give you a reason to think otherwise. See Chapter 8.)

Not a good idea.

> *trustworthy* \ trast **wer** thee \: *a compound word in the English language meaning worthy of being trusted. A person who, by their actions and attitudes, has earned the right to be trusted to hold you in safe keeping.*

So tell me how you can know another person is trustworthy? Make sure you understand it clearly. Do you know how to determine whether another person is worthy of your trust, really? And how do you know the person who wronged you is worthy of trusting them again?

> "Well, it's when … it's when … ummm … they do what they say they'll do?"

Not easy to explain is it? Let me give an example to help you understand and determine whether a person is indeed worthy of your trust. It's in the form of a three-legged stool:

> Leg one. What they *say* and what they *do* match … over a long period of time. Their words match their actions.

> Leg two. What they *say today* and what they *say tomorrow* match … over a long period of time. Their words match their words.

> Leg three. What they *do today* and what they *do tomorrow* match … over a long period of time. Their actions match their actions.

With each leg of the stool there's a consistency and a constancy in their words and actions AND both are lived out over a long period of time.

Anybody can make their words and actions match for a short time. We see this all the time with con-artists, domestic violence perpetrators and other offenders. Anybody can make their story the same for a short period of time. We see this all the time with manipulators and liars. Anybody can make their actions stay the same for a short period of time. People with addictions do this over and over again. It's over the *long haul* they show their true intentions.

TRUST IS EARNED, NOT GIVEN

No, I'm not paranoid. This is the truth. The mistake made in relationships all the time (I see this especially between parents and their teenager) is you *want* the other person to be trustworthy so you decide to trust them so they'll become trustworthy.

No. It doesn't make any sense at all.

> "You just gotta trust me with the car, Dad! How else can I show you that you can trust me?"

No, dad/parent. Trust has to be earned ... not given. Not trusting ... yet ... is not the same as being paranoid or overly-anxious. It's being observant and aware.

> "But she's my supervisor so I have to trust her ... Don't I?"

You need to *respect* her as your supervisor, yes. Trust her just because she's your supervisor? Not unless she's trustworthy. Just because a person has a title, position, rank, status or role does not make them trustworthy. Yes, you "salute the rank not the person," but that's not the same as trusting.

Trust must be earned.

If you're a supervisor and reading this, I will willingly give you the respect you organizationally deserve as my boss. However, it's on your shoulders to earn my trust ... or not earn it, your choice.

130

Trust is too important to our emotional and mental health to just, "give it," to another person. Way too important. It has to be earned.

Wrong Question

When the issue of trusting comes up, it's often in the form of a question, "You do trust me, don't you?" or "How can I trust them after what they did to me?"

Wrong question.

The issue is *not* a matter of *you* trusting *them*. The burden is *not* on your shoulders for anything. It's *not* your job to trust them. The broken trust is *not* yours to fix or remedy.

Not at all.

The issue is; are *they* trustworthy? Are *they* worthy of *you* trusting them to hold you in safe keeping? The burden is on *their* shoulders for all of it. It's *their* job to become worthy of your trust. Since *they* broke the trust, it's totally *theirs* to fix or remedy by becoming trustworthy.

These are the questions we need to be asking. These are the right questions to ask. That's the healthy question and that's the safe question.

Stomping on the Ice

> "The person who wronged me used to be trustworthy, they really were. But how do I know when they're trustworthy again? I mean, they don't normally do things like that. Are they supposed to lose all my trust?"

Let me share a story. I moved to Colorado to take a position at a youth camp that had a lake [1]. In the winter and into the spring we would play ice hockey on the frozen lake. It was there I learned how to judge whether ice was safe enough to hold my weight or not.

"How can you tell if it's safe?"

First, you stand on the bank—where you're safe—evaluate (observe) the ice, its condition and its texture. You look for soggy patches and cracks.

> Then, with one foot still on the bank, you take your other foot and stomp on the ice as far out as you can reach without losing your balance.

>> If it holds and sounds solid, you take a few steps out—where you're safe—lean out and stomp again.

>>> If it's solid, you take a few more steps out—where you're safe—and stomp again.

>>>> If it holds solid, you know the ice is safe enough. You know you can trust the ice to hold your weight.

That's what you do with another person—not literally stomp on them, I mean—you take little steps of testing; small steps until they *prove* themselves worthy of your trust. This process takes time and can't be rushed. Remember the story of Joseph and how he tested his brothers—several times—before he let them know he was their brother? Joseph was stomping on ice even in Egypt.

> "But, he has so much potential to be a good person. He can become trustworthy."

Fine. But has he earned your trust *today*?

> "But ..."

No, is he worthy of you trusting him right *now*?

> "But, I see improvement. He's a lot better than what he used to be."

132

Okay, but the issue is not what you *want* him to be, it's what he *is*. Sure, physically beating you only three times per week is an "improvement" from five times per week like he used to but … he's still not safe *now*.

Is he safe *today*? Is he worthy of you trusting him *today*?

If he hasn't earned your trust *today*—you *don't trust* him *today*.

If he becomes worthy of your trust in the future—you can trust him in the future—but *not* today.

Who's working harder at this trustworthy status, you or him? Sounds to me like you may be and it's not up to you to fix this. It's totally his responsibility to become a person worthy of your trust and be that three-legged stool we discussed.

The hard part for you comes if the person you *want* to trust so badly, chooses *not* to be a trustworthy person and you're left without that person to trust.

> "I don't know if I can handle that."

Then talk with a mental health professional or a qualified person, but you still don't trust that person.

Trusting for Real

---

trust \ trust \: *better understood as entrust (a) to confidently commit or place your safe-keeping into the hands of another; (b) to rely on the trustworthiness of another person—to believe them.*

Back to the topic of forgiving. The offending person wronged you. You forgive the debt. But are they worthy of being trusted? Were they truly worthy of your trust before this wrong happened?

Remember the example of you getting mad at me, finding my car in the parking lot and breaking out my windshield?

Step One – Breaking my windshield is wrong.

Step Two – You owe me a new windshield.

Step Three – I gave *Other* the debt.

Step Four – My copy is marked "PAID IN FULL."

The gavel drops.

Court is adjourned.

Step Five – I fix my own windshield. I pay (absorb) the cost. I suffer.

Yes, I did forgive you ... but I'm *not* telling you where I park my car! I don't trust you because you broke the trust I had in you.

How do I know you're worthy of my trust again?

I don't.

At this point, you're *not* trustworthy.

So I don't trust you ... yet.

Entrust is an active, present tense verb meaning it's now, right here, in this moment. Trustworthy needs to be viewed in the same active present tense, now, right here, in this moment, when evaluating. Maybe in the future I can trust the offender after trust has been re-earned and re-established. Maybe never. I don't know ... but I do know it's not today.

"Oh, but how do I live in a marriage with a person who isn't trustworthy? That's my situation."

Not easy to do. I've worked with a number of clients who were in marriages where that was the case. I've worked with many parents who have to share custody with an ex-spouse who's not trustworthy.

Think of it this way, if you are an ambassador and you're having dinner with the president of a country who's a sworn enemy of yours, how do you behave? Would you trust them? But you have to interact with them. How would you behave?

"Yikes. I'm not sure how I'd behave."

You'd be polite, guarded, you'd be superficial. You'd stick to the topics that are safe to discuss and then you'd get the heck out of there.

Sadly, that's how you live if your spouse is not trustworthy. You keep your guard up. You look out for yourself. You don't trust. You keep things on a superficial level and keep your distance as needed.

"Above all else, guard you heart, for it is the wellspring of life" [2].

"But that's no way to have a marriage."

I agree yet that's how you function and keep yourself safe if that's the marriage you're in. And ... if that spouse is *not* a safe person to be around, you may need to think how to get far enough away—emotionally and physically—so you don't keep getting hurt. That's a topic worthy of a book all its own.

And, if it's your ex-, you do the same and keep the interactions as short, polite and businesslike as you can. If need be, only meet in public areas with other people close by. Not easy to do, still, that's what you do.

Angie

You've followed Angie's story for a long time now, what do you think she did?

"She forgave her parents but didn't trust either of them."

Correct. That's not an easy thing for a teenage girl to do. And when she could—at the age of 18—she left the home and took care of herself.

You can forgive and still not trust.

Why Trust?

What's a good reason to trust another person? What's the reason for doing so? What good does it do?

"Well, because you're supposed to ... I think."

And who says you're "supposed" to?

When it comes to trusting there's lots of questions we just don't ask and I'm not sure why. Trust is such an important topic you would think we'd be asking more questions about it. Instead, it seems, we talk all around it but never ask the hard questions.

So what *is* the real reason for trusting another person (if they're trustworthy)?

So why, "confidently commit your safe-keeping into the hands of another"?

First, so you don't have to walk through life alone. Doing life alone—physically, emotionally and/or spiritually—is very difficult to do. Think of all the human interactions you rely on just to get through an ordinary day. Imagine if you were "all alone" and had to do the same day's activities. People do it. The ones who have to—by no real choice of their own—tell me it's very stressful, wearing and lonely.

One of the reasons to entrust your safekeeping into another person's hands is explained in the following sayings of a wise ancient king:

"Two are better than one, because they have a good reward for their toil. For if they fall, one will lift up his fellow. But woe to him who is alone when he falls and has not another to lift him up!" [3]

"If two lie together, they keep warm, but how can one keep warm alone?"[4]

"A man might prevail against one who is alone, two will withstand him" [5]

If you place your trust in another person, you have two minds to solve problems, you have two sets of hands to complete the task and you have somebody who "has your back" as we say.

The second reason for trusting—a trustworthy person—is to have a relationship with another human being. Human beings are designed as relational beings and relating deeply takes trust. You can chit-chat with another person without any real trusting going on, but chit-chat only goes so deep. You can talk about facts and events without requiring much in the way of trusting the other person. It probably won't cost you anything—physically or psychologically—if you get into a disagreement over simple facts and events.

"My name's Tim. You're alive today. We're living on planet earth. I'm the author of this book."

It will be hard to attack me over any of these statements. I have very little risk of being humiliated/hurt by you. I'm not risking much because I'm not really putting much of myself into your hands for safe keeping, am I?

When we talk about our ideas, opinions and thoughts, we begin to risk a little more … and gain a little more insight into each other as well. I'm beginning to put a little bit of myself into your hands—because it's *my* thoughts, *my* opinions—to either "keep safe" or hurt me by making fun of or disagreeing with my ideas, etc.

"I think I did a really good job writing this book."

Hear it? I just opened myself up to show more of myself. I also opened myself up to be disagreed with and made fun of/critiqued by you.

By the time we begin talking about *my* dreams, *my* deep desires, hopes and longings, I'm putting a larger and larger part of myself out there—into your hands—that you can either keep safe or use what you know against me to hurt me. You can really make fun of me now, disagreeing with me or (you name a way that you can break my trust).

The deeper we go in sharing ourselves—the more I entrust myself to you and you to me—the more deeply the connecting and bonding grows between us. If you're trustworthy I feel appreciated and cared for by you.

Trusting another person sets the stage for deep, personal and intimate connecting, caring, validating, supporting and protecting. This is the stuff we need to live fulfilled and complete lives. That's the reason to go through the time and hassle of "stomping on the ice" with another person to see if they're worth entrusting part—or all—of yourself into their hands for safe keeping.

That's why you trust.

That's also why you trust very slowly and only after the person has earned your trust.

Workbook Session

Trust and Trustworthy- and Restoring

What do you think it means to *trust* another person?

_____

_____

_____

_____

_____

_____

_____

How would you explain what *trustworthy* is to another person?

_____

_____

_____

_____

_____

_____

_____

_____

_____

"Trust is earned, not given." What are your thoughts about saying trust has to be earned?

_____

_____

_____

_____

_____

_____

_____

_____

Have you ever trusted a person who ended up not being trustworthy? Looking back, what warning signs do you see now that would have alerted you to their un-trustworthiness?

_____

_____

_____

_____

_____

_____

_____

_____

_____

_____

_____

_____

Head and Heart Check:

If you're a person who trusts too easily or naïvely, why do you think that is? What are you attempting to gain—or avoid—by giving your trust to another so easily? Are you aware you do this?

_____

_____

_____

_____

_____

_____

_____

_____

_____

What do you need to see in/from the person who wronged you to determine whether they're trustworthy or not (again or for the first time)?

_____

_____

_____

_____

_____

_____

_____

_____

_____

If you're a person who doesn't trust other people, what would it take for you to trust a (trustworthy) person?

_____

_____

_____

_____

_____

_____

_____

_____

_____

If you're a person who trusts wisely, how would you describe the benefits of trusting to a person who's afraid to trust?

_____

_____

_____

_____

_____

_____

_____

_____

_____

_____

_____

Restoring

While not the focus of this book, here are some questions to consider if all has gone well to this point between you and the person who wronged you.

What steps need to happen between you and the person who wronged you in order for the relationship to be restored?

_____

_____

_____

_____

_____

_____

_____

_____

Do you want it restored? Why or why not?

_____

_____

_____

_____

_____

_____

_____

_____

_____

What do you need to see in the person before you know it's safe for you to attempt to restore the relationship?

_____

_____

_____

_____

_____

_____

_____

Do you feel pressure from the person or other people to restore the relationship even if you don't want to? Who are those people?

_____

_____

_____

_____

_____

_____

What reasons do those people give as to why you "have" to restore the relationship?

_____

_____

_____

_____

_____

_____

What do you need to do to keep yourself strong and safe if you choose not to restore the relationship?

_____

_____

_____

_____

_____

_____

_____

_____

_____

_____

_____

What will be the benefits of a restored relationship with this person?

_____

_____

_____

_____

_____

_____

_____

Chapter Eleven

Coming Full Circle

You can forgive without confronting.

You can confront without being reconciled.

You can reconcile without trusting.

You can trust without restoring the relationship.

Restoring the relationship means:

You have forgiven that person ...
The other person is safe enough to interact with ...
When you confronted the person they confessed—gave an apology—and offered what restitution could be offered ...
The two of you reconciled ...
The other person is living a trustworthy life for a long enough period of time ...

And ...

You *choose* to rebuild the relationship. You're not obligated to, you choose to.

Then and only then can the relationship move in the direction of being restored—put back together—between the two of you.

Then ... and ... *only* then.

So that's it. That's what forgiving is. That's the journey—the court procedure— involved in forgiving the person who wronged you.

"So, where does that leave me now?"

We've come full circle. Remember the word picture of walking through our hospital full of hurting people? Here we are again. The hurt and damage is legitimate. No, it's not "all in your head." The hurt is real. The wrong did take place; that's why you're in the hospital in the first place. Forgiving is not cheap, quick or easy, remember?

Theologically, forgive means:

> TO LIFT OFF the weight of the debt,
> to SEND IT AWAY from you,
> and to ABSORB the damage or injury yourself.

Psychologically, forgive means:

> TO LIFT OFF the weight of the debt,
> to SEND IT AWAY from you,
> and to ABSORB the damage or injury yourself.

Forgiving is identifying the wrong done against you ...

> Acknowledging the debt the offending person owes to you ...

> > Giving the debt collecting job over to *Other* ...

> > > Remembering, the person doesn't owe you now ...

> > > > Doing what you need to do to (absorb the damage) in order to heal and move on ...

> > > > > And not reminding the person of the wrong they did against you.

The act of forgiving that person their wrong against you doesn't heal you. It sets you up so you *can* heal ... now ... from this point forward ... in a real and complete way. I turn you over to the many books, seminars and therapists that address the healing process. There's no need to re-write what's been written so well other places.

Angie was able to forgive her father. You can forgive the person who wronged you too, even if the wrong was horrendous and extremely damaging.

Yes, you *can* heal. Yes, you *will* heal. It will probably take longer than you wish, that's all. Don't force your journey into a timeline or formula. If you're helping somebody else with their forgiving process, respect them and remind them this process takes "heart time."

You can FORGIVE FOR REAL.

Workbook Session

Coming Full Circle

You can forgive without confronting.

You can confront without being reconciled.

You can reconcile without trusting.

You can trust without restoring the relationship.

If you've worked through all the steps and the relationship is restored, or being restored ... you've come full circle. What steps do you need to take to help yourself finish healing and, going back to the hospital word picture, be discharged?

_____

_____

_____

_____

_____

_____

_____

_____

_____

_____

_____

Head and Heart Check:

Are you prone to being a, *"victim"*, rather than seeing yourself as a person who was, *"victimized"*? If so, why do you see yourself that way? What benefit does playing the victim have for you?

_____

_____

_____

_____

_____

_____

In Summary

This is the journey called forgiving. These are the steps to take to walk that journey. A journey that will be measured in *heart time*, and can take significant chronological time to complete.

If you've completed your journey, congratulations!

If you're the person who's helping another person with their forgiving journey, please be patient with that person.

My hope is to get every person through the "courtroom" and out of the "hospital" with debts PAID IN FULL and as healed as possible. I hope that's been the case for you.

APPENDIX

How to Ask to be Forgiven

While not specifically part of the, "forgiving", journey, it's worth a quick look at how you ask somebody you wronged to forgive you. When you realize you've wronged another person, it's *your* responsibility to initiate asking them to forgive you [1]. Much of what we've already talked about applies here.

How to Ask

It's better to ask to be forgiven face-to-face for the same reasons it's better to confront face-to-face. Again, Skype and/or phone contact are acceptable in a pinch if meeting in person isn't possible. I would stress not to ask through written communication (a letter, email or text message) again for the same reasons I suggested not to confront in written form.

When you ask to be forgiven, you are offering the confession—the apology—as laid out in Chapter Three. Here's that outline again:

> You (the offending person) state:
>
> "I ..." a personal admission that you were the offending person.
>
> "did this ..." a clear confession of the action that took place.
>
> "against you ..." a clear admission that they are the offended person.

"it was wrong ..." a clear admission that the action was actually wrong.

"it hurt you ..." a statement acknowledging the wrong action had a damaging and negative affect on the person you're asking forgiveness from.

"and I will make what restitution I can." A statement accepting the legitimate debt incurred that is yours to pay.

Rehearse what you will say beforehand. You may want to make up an outline to follow when you ask for forgiveness.

Stick to the facts—the courtroom procedure and documents—and, once again, let me encourage you to keep yourself as un-emotional and objective as you can when asking. Asking them to forgive you can be kept to about four or five sentences. Keep it short and to the point. If the conversation is successful, you may choose to go on and mend the relationship and emotions are very acceptable and welcomed at that point.

After you ask, be quiet. Wait. Give the offended person time to process your request and consider their response. As hard as it may be to wait, don't hurry their response. Wait for them to either *accept* or *reject* your request.

Accept whatever response the person gives you. Don't try to *make* them forgive you. There's no need to ask again. There's no reason to beg or plead to be forgiven. There's no need to press them to forgive you. Now, it's up to the offended person to decide what they will do because the decision has been given to them to accept or deny your request.

As with confronting, have a plan in place to end the conversation and go your way. This will be especially important if the conversation does not go well. It's a way of keeping yourself safe.

If They Accept

If the offended person accepts your apology:

Determine whether there's any restitution you can legitimately offer. If there is, then make arrangements to do so. If there isn't, then there isn't.

With your confession offered and accepted, both sides are saying the same thing and you are reconciled. From here, the matter of trusting and whether the other person wants to begin relationship mending is up to them. Your job of asking them to forgive you is complete.

If They Refuse

If the offended person *refuses* to accept your apology, the conversation is over. You did what you came to do and all that's your responsibility to do. It's not your job to make sure they accept your request. Not at all. There's nothing more for you to do. Politely end the conversation and go on your way. There's no need to beg, plead or repeat yourself.

Tango

> "They wronged me too. It takes two to tango, you know. Shouldn't they ask me to forgive them for what *they* did to me?"

Simply, no. You're expecting and/or hoping they will apologize to you too. It's not your place to expect that or the correct motivation to ask for forgiveness.

> "But, I *want* them to ask me for my forgiveness too."

Okay, but no. All that's yours to do is to address the wrong *you* did against them. Period. Besides, have you worked through Chapter Two to see if what they did was really a wrong? Be careful. Own your own wrongs, not the other person's wrongs. Don't try to tell them what to do with their wrong. It's theirs, not yours.

"But they really *did* wrong me."

Okay, but don't expect, hope for, or press them to reciprocate. These are two separate cases in two separate court hearings and need to be kept separate.

Let's say the other person *does* turn around and ask you to forgive them for the wrong they did against you, great. Let me make this suggestion; make sure your request is completed and finished *before* changing the conversation to their request of you. Follow the court procedures. It will be better all-around to have a clear end to one conversation and a clear start to the second. It will be helpful for you and them on both counts.

Now, follow the steps and accept their apology.

Not Safe

Safety is a theme throughout this book, have you noticed? That's very intentional because it's something you need to always remember and not assume is present. So again, what if the person you wronged is *not* a safe person to approach?

"What do I do then?"

You can do something symbolic in place of a face-to-face encounter much like we talked about doing when it's not safe to confront the person. Write a letter of confession—apology—to the person. Read this letter to your therapist, your dog, your priest, an empty chair you envision the person sitting in, a trusted friend or **Other**. Then take the letter and destroy it. How you chose to do that is up to you. If you need to keep it so you can remind yourself you did ask to be forgiven, then keep it. Write the date on and put it someplace safe.

"Above all else, guard your heart ..."

Can't Ask?

> "But what if I can't find the person I wronged, or what if they're dead now?"

In cases like this—which I see on a regular basis in my practice—follow the process above in the situation where the person is not safe to approach. If you're not a letter writer, that's fine. Set up a situation where you can talk it out. The empty chair technique can be helpful at times like this. Whatever works for you. There's no "right way" to do this.

Can't or Won't?

The, "I can't ask because ..." is sometimes used as an excuse when you can't accept the reality you could (did) actually wrong somebody that way. You can't envision yourself, "stooping that low," to actually ask the person—when it is safe and possible—to forgive you. Asking for forgiveness makes your action more real than you want to own up to. Denying the wrong and believing that not asking forgiveness helps you save face is a form of seeing yourself and the situation inaccurately—not reality.

Remember, sanity is when your perception of yourself and the reality about yourself *match*. Yes, it can be very humbling to go to the person and ask them to forgive you. Embrace/accept the truth about yourself and deal with the wrong you did. It's always more freeing than holding on to your illusion of yourself no matter how good that illusion feels.

Angie

After helping Angie work through forgiving her father, I asked if there was anything she had done during the fight that was a wrong against her father.

> "What! She doesn't have to ask to be forgiven of anything. Her father's the one doing the wrong!"

Not always so.

As we talked through the events of the fight, Angie realized a couple of things she said to her father were wrong.

Yes, her father's physical assault of Angie was a huge wrong.

Yes, his yelling and saying the things he did to her was wrong.

And—in the midst of all the wrong things her father was doing to her—Angie remembers cursing her father several times.

Is cursing another person wrong? A moral wrong, yes. So, in the middle of all the wrongs her father was doing—which we never minimized—did she commit an offense against her father?

> "Well, yes, but don't tell me you made her go and ask her father to forgive her. You didn't, did you?"

We worked through the steps of making a true apology for the wrong she did against her father. She wrote out an apology using the steps suggested earlier.

I then asked her if she thought it was safe enough for her to ask her father to forgive her face-to- face. We talked this question over for a couple of sessions. It's not a question for Angie—or anyone—to take lightly. Is this person *safe* enough to approach in person and ask to be forgiven?

Angie finally decided she wanted to go to her father and ask him to forgive her. We made sure she was asking forgiveness for *only* the things she did; the cursing. We made sure she didn't take the blame or the fault for the entire fight or for her black eye. We kept her outline short and to the point. When we finalized what she was going to say, she asked me to pray for her because she was going to talk to her father that coming week.

The next week, she told me she'd done what she set out to do; she asked her father to forgive her for the cursing she'd done against him.

> "Why did you let her talk to that man? You said he
> *wasn't* safe enough to confront. Why did you let a
> teenage girl go up against her angry father? Why?"

Yes, it was *not* safe for Angie to *confront* her father. When it
came to asking him to forgive her we both figured her father
would see Angie's confession as a "victory" over his daughter
and accept her apology without incident.

He did exactly that.

He acted very civil and told Angie, "thank you for being such a
wise daughter" … blah … blah … blah … (which neither Angie
nor I believed) and the conversation ended well.

> "But *why*? He's a jerk and he wasn't sincere at all … and
> …"

I fully agree.

Angie decided she wanted to do this because then she knew,
before her God, she did what was asked of her. There was
nothing left for her to do and she could walk away in confidence.

What she didn't expect was she also walked away from that
conversation feeling vindicated. She realized she was the "bigger
person" and that she'd chosen to do that herself … for herself.
Even though her father chose the path of denial and living in
"insanity", she chose the higher road. She chose the path of
honesty, health and healing. It boosted her self-confidence more
than either of us expected and in doing so, helped her to heal
more quickly and become an even stronger person … as a
teenager.

> "Way to go Angie!"

> Amen to that!

What does "Forgive Myself" Mean?

One comment on a phrase that's not part of how you forgive somebody else but it often gets spoken in conjunction with forgiving. That phrase is, *"Now all I have to do is find a way to forgive myself."*

Not to belabor the point, but what are you forgiving yourself for doing to you? In light of what forgiving actually is, what wrong did you do against yourself? What law did you break that created an offense against *yourself*?

What do you actually mean by, "I need to forgive myself?"

"You know, forgive myself."

Do you need to take yourself to court and say, *"Your honor, I wronged myself and I owe myself this debt and I need to forgive me for the debt I owe me?"*

After hearing countless people try to describe what they mean when they use this phrase, I began researching its origin. Nowhere in the Bible does it describe anybody forgiving themselves or encouraging the reader to do so. Nowhere in my graduate studies—or studies afterward—have I come across any psychological research evaluating this action or actual outcome of "forgiving yourself."

So, somewhere somebody coined the phrase and it stuck in our culture. There were five ideas that kept reoccurring as I did my research. Here's what I think the real meaning is behind the phrase, *"I have to forgive myself."* I'll describe each briefly and you can see if one of these is more in line with what you mean if/when you use the phrase.

False Guilt

When you offend (different than wronged) another person, you can carry around what people commonly call false guilt: feelings of sorrow, embarrassment, shame, sadness and/or disappointment about what happened. You may have the *feeling* of being guilty for doing something, "wrong," you may have the *perception* of being at fault, but you're not guilty of any real offense. Not really. So the sense of being guilty is a false sense. The feelings are real but aren't related whatsoever with being guilty.

Like described early in the book, forgiveness is a legal-type process and sticks to the facts of what you actually did wrong—breaking of a civil or moral law—against another person. You can't have a *feeling* of a charge of guilty. Being guilty is a statement of *fact*. The *feeling* you are experiencing may be better expressed by using a word such as:

> Embarrassed
> Disappointed
> Grief
> Emotional pain
> Sad
> Sorrowful

Think over this list of feeling words and see if what you're trying to express can more accurately be described using one of these words.

Aftermath of True Guilt

When you are truly guilty of an offense against another person, you don't know what to do with the *feelings* that are associated with the wrong. You are experiencing an emotion—or several emotions collectively—that may fit more accurately into one of these words again:

> Embarrassed
> Disappointed
> Grief
> Emotional pain

Sad
Sorrowful

Guilty is not a feeling. You may experience emotions that linger after you've asked to be forgiven and/or offered restitution. The court charge of guilty has been absolved but you still have *feelings* related to the event. Again, one of the words may more accurately describe what you're experiencing and attempting to verbalize.

Needs to Soak In

Let's say you were guilty of a wrong action against another person. Again, it's a statement of fact not a feeling. Another *fact* is—let's say—you were forgiven. For whatever reason it's hard for you to accept the other person's forgiving of you. Could it be you have a hard time accepting anything from another person?

Maybe it's your pride that won't allow you to admit you would "stoop that low" as to actually wrong another person in that manner. We talked about this before, remember? Something inside you, keeps fighting the reality—the fact—that you *are* forgiven. Before settling on, *"I have to forgive myself,"* ask yourself if you need to adjust your *perception* of yourself to match the *reality* of yourself; you were forgiven by another person. It's over. Accept the fact. Allow that truth—and the ramifications of that truth—to be real and soak into your mind and heart.

Wounded Deeply

Maybe you're wounded so deeply—for any number of reasons— you're drowning in a sea of shame and don't know how to get rid of the shame and self-contempt ... or don't even know what to call it. It may be you carry around so much shame you can't fathom the fact that you're even *worthy* to be forgiven. Guilt is a fact of doing a wrong action. Shame is a perception of yourself that states, *"I'm bad, broken, undeserving of any anything good."* Shame can devour our entire being—even though it's not true.

But it feels so true.

But it's not true about you.

> But it feels so true it feels it really is you. Not something you *did*, but it's who you *are*.

Please, if you've been deeply wounded and/or thinking, *"I'm just bad, broken, undeserving of anything good"*, sounds all too familiar, find somebody you can talk to or begin reading about shame, how to identify it and what to start doing about it. Shame may be one of the things lurking behind the phrase, *"I need to forgive myself."*

You Were Taught

Lastly, it may be simply that you were taught you need to, *"forgive yourself,"* that's what you're supposed to do. But nobody explained the what and why of forgiving yourself or if that was even an actual thing for you to do. If this is your reason for using this phrase, it may be time to learn something different, something more accurate.

It could be one of these descriptions more accurately describes what you truly mean to say when saying, *"I need to forgive myself."*

As good as it sounds, I don't believe it actually exists or is a legitimate action you need to take. I challenge you to think over the scenarios and words listed above to see of one of these is a more accurate explanation of what you're attempting to say. It can be very freeing to finally put accurate word(s) with what that feeling is inside.

Very freeing.

Workbook Session

Appendix

Asking to be Forgiven

Again, while not the main focus of the book, it's very natural to begin to consider situations in which you may need to ask to be forgiven for an offense you've committed. Here are the worksheets for that journey should you need to take this step. You'll find many of the "court proceedings" are the same as you've worked through already.

Use Worksheet 6

When you realize *you've* wronged another person, it's your responsibility to initiate and ask them to forgive you. Is there anything you've done to wrong another person? If so, put the person's name down on Worksheet 6.

Put the name of the person you wronged (go through the following Worksheets one person at a time) on Worksheet 6 and put it at the top of a Worksheet 7 page. Again, one person per page for each name listed on Worksheet 6.

Use Worksheet 7

Like you did on Worksheet 2, list the specific wrong actions you did against that person.

Test It:

What civil law was broken?

What moral law or code was transgressed?

If what you wrote down doesn't qualify, cross it off your list. If it was something foolish or stupid you did, you'll need to *address* it with that person—talk about it and try to settle things—but you won't need to ask them to forgive you for that action.

Mark It:

For each legitimate wrong you have left on Worksheet 7, off to the side, mark it with a **C** for a civil wrong and/or an **M** for a moral wrong. Carefully think through the specific action to determine the wrong done.

Use Worksheet 8

Like you did on Worksheet 3, write out what you believe you owe the person in restitution for each wrong you committed against them.

It's possible some of what you owe the person you've already provided in restitution. If you have done so already, put a **P** (paid) next to the debt that's been taken care of, then cross it off the list.

Is the person you're considering approaching safe enough to ask them to forgive you? What makes you think they're safe? What makes you think they may not be safe?

_____

_____

_____

_____

_____

_____

_____

_____

If you determined the person *is* safe enough to approach, write out what you are going to say. Remember to keep it short, concise – stick to the point.

Angie:

> "I (Angie) cursed at you (Father).
>
> It was wrong, and it hurt you.
>
> I owe this apology (confession) to you."

_____

_____

_____

_____

_____

_____

_____

_____

_____

Think through when and where you want to approach this person. Write out your plan.

_____

_____

_____

_____

_____

_____

_____

_____

_____

_____

_____

_____

_____

_____

Use Worksheet 9

How are you going to ask for forgiveness? Write out what you want to say when you ask the person to forgive you. Write it out this way:

"I (name the wrong done here)

(put their name here) it was wrong and it hurt you.

I owe you, (put their name here again): (list how you can make restitution as best as you can)."

Do you think they will *accept* or *reject* your request? What makes you think they will accept?

_____

_____

_____

_____

_____

_____

_____

_____

If they *accept*, have in mind what restitution you will provide to the person. Write down what you will offer.

_____

_____

_____

_____

_____

_____

_____

If they *reject* your request, how do you think the rejection will impact you?

_____

_____

_____

_____

_____

_____

_____

_____

What do you need to be ready to do if your request is rejected?

_____

_____

_____

_____

_____

_____

_____

If you decided the person's *not* safe enough to ask, what will you do now?

_____

_____

_____

_____

_____

_____

If you don't know where the person is or if they are alive anymore, you won't be able to ask them face to face. How can you ask them in a symbolic way that will help you move forward in your healing journey?

_____

_____

_____

_____

_____

_____

_____

_____

_____

_____

What Does "Forgive Myself" Mean?

Here are some quick questions for you to consider from the chapter regarding the phrase, "I need to forgive myself."

If you use this phrase, *"I need to forgive myself,"* what do you mean when you say it?

_____

_____

_____

_____

_____

_____

Read the possible meanings that may be behind the phrase, *"I need to forgive myself."* Which of these suggested phrases, or another you've identified, sounds more like what you mean when you use it? What do you think is behind your thinking?

_____

_____

_____

_____

_____

_____

_____

_____

How could using that phrase or idea more accurately for yourself actually help you?

_____

_____

_____

_____

_____

_____

_____

WORKSHEETS

WORKSHEET 1

Step One – The Wrong Done Against You

Using the book's definition of a wrong, write down the name of each person who has wronged you. If you're not sure what the person did was a legitimate wrong, write their name anyway, you can sort it out later.

When making your list, consider both ways the person may have wronged you by:

DOING something BAD to you.

Or …

NOT DOING something GOOD to you.

Person or persons who have wronged me:

_____

_____

_____

_____

_____

_____

_____

_____

_____

_____

_____

_____

WORKSHEET 2

Step One – The Wrong Done Against You

Name of person

_____

List all the wrongs you think this person did against you. Again, if you're not sure it was a legitimate wrong, add it to the list anyway, you can sort it out later.

Be as specific as you can. Write out the what, when, where and how for the wrong(s).

Note:

You may choose to categorize and/or generalize wrongs if the same offense was repeated multiple times or if there's a similar pattern to the wrong actions. Do whatever helps you keep things clear in your thinking.

_____

_____

_____

_____

_____

_____

_____

_____

Other wrong actions may come to mind as you work though the Workbook Sessions, that's fine, simply add them to your list.

WORKSHEET 3

Step Two – The Debt That is Owed
Step Three – Who Will be the Debt Collector?
Step Four – Paid in Full

For each wrong listed on Worksheet 2, write out what the person owes you for that wrong.

_____

_____

_____

_____

_____

_____

_____

_____

_____

_____

_____

The person can't, "make it like it never happened," because it did happen. This is restitution that the person needs to provide to pay the debt owed to you.

You will use Worksheet 3 for Step Three and Step Four

WORKSHEET 4

Step Five – Absorbing the Damage

For each wrong you listed on Worksheet 2, write out all the
damages you suffered—or are suffering—because of it. List the
tangible—as well as any intangible—damages from the wrong.
(I.e. emotional, physical, financial).

_____

_____

_____

_____

_____

_____

_____

_____

_____

_____

_____

_____

_____

_____

_____

_____

_____

_____

_____

WORKSHEET 5

People You Wronged

When making your list, consider both ways you may have wronged the other person by:

DOING something BAD to them.

Or …

NOT DOING something GOOD to them.

Person or persons who I have wronged:

_____

_____

_____

_____

_____

_____

_____

_____

_____

_____

_____

_____

_____

_____

_____

WORKSHEET 6

The Wrong You Did
Against the Person(s)

Name of person

_____

List all the wrongs you think you committed against the other
person. Again, if you're not sure it was a legitimate wrong, add
it to the list anyway, you can sort it out later.

Be as specific as you can. Write out the what, when, where and
how for the infraction(s).

_____

_____

_____

_____

_____

_____

_____

_____

_____

_____

_____

Other wrong actions may come to mind, that's fine, simply
add them to your list.

WORKSHEET 7

The Debt You Owe

For each wrong listed, write out what you owe the person because of that wrong.

_____

_____

_____

_____

_____

_____

_____

_____

_____

_____

_____

_____

_____

_____

_____

_____

_____

_____

_____

_____

You can't, "make it like it never happened," because it did happen. This is restitution you need to provide to the other person.

WORKSHEET 8

Asking to be Forgiven

Write out your confession you will use to ask the person to forgive you.

Write it out this way:

"I_____
(name the wrong done here)

_____
(put their name here)

it was wrong and it hurt you.

I owe _____
(list how you can make retribution as best as you can)

_____
(put their name here again)."

Do you think there's anything else you want/need to say to the person? If so, what do you want to say?

_____

_____

_____

_____

_____

_____

_____

_____

End Notes

Chapter One – Why Forgive?

1. Matthew 6:14-15; Mark 11:25; Luke 6:37; Ephesians 4:23; Colossians 3:13
2. John 8:32
3. To keep legal confidentiality, I have changed enough of the events and facts of this story to protect my client's true identity.
4. James Strong, S.T.D., LL.D., Strong's Exhaustive Concordance of the Bible (MacDonald Publishing Company, McLean, VA)
5. Ibid

Chapter Two – Step One – The Wrong Done Against You

1. In this actual case, mandatory reporting protocol was followed.

Chapter Four – Step Three – Who Will be the Debt Collector

1. Romans 12:19

Chapter Eight – Confronting

1. Matthew 18:15
2. Proverbs 9:7-8a
3. The context is I Corinthians 6:1-6
4. Proverbs 4:23
5. Ibid

Chapter Nine – Reconciling

1. Romans 12:18

Chapter Ten – Trust and Trustworthy

1. Eagle Lake Camp, owned and operated by The Navigators
2. Proverbs 4:23
3. Ecclesiastes 4:9-10

4. Ecclesiastes 4:11
5. Ecclesiastes 4:12

Appendix A – How to Ask to be Forgiven

1. Matthew 5:23

www.ingramcontent.com/pod-product-compliance
Lightning Source LLC
Chambersburg PA
CBHW072045280526
45788CB00006B/2184